QUICK COOKING
■ *with* ■
PACIFIC FLAVORS

QUICK COOKING
■ *with* ■
PACIFIC FLAVORS

by

HUGH CARPENTER

and

TERI SANDISON

STEWART, TABORI & CHANG

New York

Text copyright © 1997 by Hugh Carpenter
Photographs copyright © 1997 by Teri Sandison

Published in 1997 and distributed in the U. S. by
Stewart, Tabori & Chang,
a division of U.S. Media Holdings, Inc.
115 West 18th Street, New York, NY 10011

Distributed in Canada by
General Publishing Company Ltd.
30 Lesmill Road
Don Mills, Ontario, M3B 2T6, Canada

Distributed in Australia by
Peribo Pty Ltd.
58 Beaumont Road
Mount Kuring-gai, NSW 2080, Australia

Distributed in all other territories by
Grantham Book Services Ltd.
Isaac Newton Way, Alma Park Industrial Estate
Grantham, Lincolnshire, NG31 9SD, England

Library of Congress Cataloging-in-Publication Data

Carpenter, Hugh.
        Quick cooking with Pacific flavors / by Hugh Carpenter and Teri Sandison.
                p. cm
        Includes index.
        ISBN 1-55670-645-6 (hardcover)
        1. Cookery, Oriental. 2. Quick and easy cookery. I. Sandison, Teri. II. Title.
    TX724.5.A1C373   1997
    641.595—dc21   97-9785

Printed in Japan

10 9 8 7 6 5 4 3 2 1

This book is lovingly dedicated to our parents
Warwick and Peggy Carpenter and Robert and Barbara Sandison
who encouraged us to live life to the fullest.

Contents

Preface *8*

Introduction *10*

Chapter 1:

· · · · · · · · · · · ·

Wun Sum and Dim Sum *14*

Chapter 2:

· · · · · · · · · ·

Crunchy, Crispy, Crackling Salads *44*

Chapter 3:

· · · · · · · · · · · ·

New Wave Soups *66*

Chapter 4:

· · · · · · · · ·

Seafood and Meats:
Sizzling and Smoking *82*

Chapter 5:

Mu Shu Fantasies
and Stir-Fry Triumphs 108

Chapter 6:

Magical Side Dishes
for an Entrée 128

Chapter 7:

Sinful Sweets 152

All About Woks and Stir-Frying 170

Asian Ingredients and Shopping Information 172

Credits and Acknowledgments 185

Index 188

Preface

When Lena Tabori, publisher of Stewart, Tabori & Chang, asked if we would like to update our cookbook *Chopstix,* Teri and I enthusiastically agreed. Since its publication in 1990, our cooking has evolved to reflect the ongoing trend toward easy-to-find ingredients, quick-to-make recipes, and simple menus.

Throughout this book, we highlight the popular trend of using Asian seasonings to add flavor to familiar American cooking. In this substantial revision, our theme has been "simplify, clarify, and educate." We have replaced 49 of the 110 recipes with new recipes that better reflect contemporary ingredients. Recipes that used hard-to-find ingredients, such as Thai ginger and fresh lemongrass, are modified so that these ingredients are eliminated or substitutions suggested. Menu ideas, which in *Chopstix* often focused on party themes, are simplified so that the menus are easy to make for work-night meals and informal weekend gatherings. Many of the chapter introductions and recipe headnotes have been rewritten in order to provide more practical information, such as recipe variations, cooking tips, or details about preparation steps. Now all recipe directions indicate how far ahead the preparation steps can be completed. Lastly, many of the recipes we retained were retested and reworked so that lengthy ingredients lists were shortened or complex cooking steps simplified without the dishes losing their bold original flavors.

Quick Cooking with Pacific Flavors retains many classic *Chopstix* recipes, such as Rib-Eye Steaks with Ginger-Mango Salsa, Sichuan Veal Meat Loaf, Crazy Coconut Noodle Toss, and Lemon Ice Cream with Chocolate Grand Marnier. But throughout the book you will find dozens of new intensely flavored recipes. Whether it's Crisp Spring Rolls with Lettuce and Mint Wrap, Chilled Avocado Soup, or Caramel Fudge Tart with Crumble Crust, these are recipes that will excite the taste buds and make you a cooking hero with a minimum of effort.

The Asian impact on American food only hints at the vast changes that will enrich our gastronomic lives in the coming years. Between 1980 and 1990, over 3.8 million Asians immigrated to the United States, and the total Asian population rose from 1.5 percent to 2.9 percent. By the year 2050, Asians will comprise more than 10 percent of America's population. Asian restaurants are proliferating in communities across the U.S., and a flood of Asian cookbooks reinforces this ongoing trend. American chefs eat at Asian restaurants, search Asian markets for new ingredients, and fuse these into an eclectic "American" cuisine. Newspaper food sections feature articles on regional Asian food. Supermarkets devote increasing space to Asian ingredients, with a growing number of supermarkets having sushi bars and Chinese wok centers as part of their food courts. American tourism to Asia increases yearly; chefs fax recipe ideas from continent to continent; and Asian condiments, tropical fruits, and produce unknown to Americans just two decades ago are commonplace.

We hope these recipes and photographs, prepared with love and presented with enthusiasm, delight the senses and convey the same joy we feel when sharing this food with family and friends.

Hugh Carpenter and Teri Sandison
Napa Valley, 1997

Introduction

The easy-to-prepare dishes in this book have provided us with many hours of pleasure at the dining table, whether served simply, for just the two of us, or more elaborately, when we have entertained family and friends. The fresh flavors, ease of preparation, and exciting combination of Asian and American ingredients may, as it has for us, forever change the way you think about cooking and eating. Begin this love affair by serving only one of these recipes as part of a simple meal. For example, try Hot and Sour Sichuan Tomato Soup with crusty sourdough bread, or Thai-High Barbecued Chicken accompanied by baked potatoes, or braised veal shanks served with Asian Noodle Magic.

As passion builds and the urge for a more intense affair with Pacific flavors rises to the surface, move on to a dinner based on the book's recipes. Keep the menu simple by choosing just a few dishes and balancing them between do-ahead recipes and one or two requiring a little last-minute attention. By completing the salad dressing, marinades, sauces, and dessert a day ahead, you can offer a dinner that avoids turning you into a kitchen slave or transforming the meal into a culinary sprint between stove and table. The most successful dinners for us have been menus that consist of just one appetizer, then a meat or seafood entrée served with one of the side dishes from Chapter 6, next a salad course from Chapter 2, and to conclude the dinner, one of the book's marvelous desserts.

ABOUT THE RECIPES

A suggested menu is offered with nearly every recipe. Skim through the book to review the menus and you'll find many party ideas for serving Pacific flavors. In addition, keep in mind the following:

Before beginning to prepare a dish, read the entire recipe for important menu advice and information about successfully completing the recipe.

Review the ingredients list for special supplies. Essential Asian supplies are listed on page 172. Purchase the best brands listed.

When the word *minced* appears, chop the item so finely it resembles a puree. To speed the process, use an electric minichopper. This is the most timesaving piece of equipment introduced since the food processor.

It is unnecessary to peel ginger root unless the skin is wrinkled. But ginger root is very fibrous and needs to be minced in a specific way to prevent long ginger fibers from being included in a dish. The ginger fibers, or "strings," run lengthwise along the root. Always cut the ginger crosswise in paper-thin slices. Then finely mince the ginger by hand or in a food processor or minichopper.

When grated or minced citrus peel is called for, use just the outside colored skin, or zest. Grating the peel is an awful chore. Fortunately, the zest can be removed quickly with a little tool called a zester, available at cookware shops. Once the peel has been zested, it takes little time to complete the mincing.

*"Bungalow Teapot" by ceramic
artist David Gurney.*

When recipes call for minced herbs, such as cilantro, mint, or basil, always mince the herbs by hand. Food processors and minichoppers tear and bruise the herbs, causing them to turn black.

Every recipe states what can be prepared ahead of time and what needs to be done at the last moment, under the headings Advance Preparation and Last-Minute Cooking. Use these as a guide for selecting recipes and planning your cooking.

Some recipes have sauces thickened with a mixture of cornstarch and water. Add only a small amount of the mixture and bring the sauce to a low boil. Stir in a little more if the sauce does not lightly glaze your spoon. You will never need to add all the cornstarch mixture.

At the end of cooking, the words *taste and adjust seasonings* mean that this is the time to make any adjustments in flavor, rather than having your guests do it at the dining room table.

In terms of recipe serving quantities, we assume entrées will be accompanied by rice or noodles and a salad. Unless otherwise stated, all dishes can be doubled or tripled, except the stir-fry dishes. When doubling a stir-fry, have a friend simultaneously stir-fry the second portion in another wok, following your every move.

WHAT DRINKS TO SERVE

Matching the proper drink with food accents the special flavors of both the food and the drink and brings to the foreground understated, alluring flavors. Most of the recipes do not provide a specific recommendation for what to drink. Many of the books' assertively flavored Pacific-style recipes will overwhelm the subtlety of a fine white or red wine. For example, serving a beef dish seasoned with a generous amount of Asian chile sauce ruins a Cabernet Sauvignon by greatly accenting the tannins in the wine. Match spicy food with iced tea, dark beer, Champagne, and any moderately priced sake meant to be served heated. Assertively seasoned foods having little or no chile are excellent with light-bodied beers, dry to slightly sweet sakes, German Riesling Kabinetts, California Sauvignon Blancs, French Chenin Blancs, and dry Rieslings (for seafood) and with Zinfandels, Pinot Noirs, and Merlots (for red meat).

About the Photography

By Teri Sandison

I am happy to be part of a new generation of photographers that has been attracted to a career in food photography because of the possibility of artistic expression. My passion is to capture on film the meeting of food and art, and to do this with the same sense of creativity, freedom, and excitement that fuels the art movement in Los Angeles and San Francisco. The photographs in this book are portraits of recipes that Hugh and I love. I listened to Hugh conceptualize the recipes, tasted them in our kitchen, listened to the reaction of Hugh's students, and read the drafts for the book. From this personal, very intimate involvement, I created portraits to capture the essence of his food.

All the photos involve the same psychological process as for painting. I enter the studio in the morning and spend all day building a set from a blank white table, composing with color, light, and texture, and recording the "food art" on film rather than on canvas. The photos actually start weeks earlier as sketches in my notebook, beginning with the design of the food and then working outward until every inch of the page has been composed.

Next, I go to art galleries, artists' studios, tile shops, and marble showrooms looking for the right props to accent an aspect of the food, such as its texture, color, or key ingredient. Many of the tabletop artists whose ceramic, glassware, flatware, and hand-painted tablecloths appear in this book have a painting background. Their freehand drawings and their use of bright, tropical colors reflect the Pacific rim countries. Their art fits perfectly with the color combinations, textural contrasts, and flavor surprises of Hugh's food.

Often, to tie the food and contemporary tabletop art together, I paint backgrounds using watercolors, pastels, or oils. A food stylist comes to my studio to prepare the recipes for the camera. Using the freshest ingredients available from markets and gardens, we endeavor to capture on film the tastes of each of Hugh's recipes. No matter how much advance planning has been done, however, there is always a magical moment when the photo begins to take on a life of its own under the lights and camera. The scene then demands the refinements in lighting, composition or food styling that make the difference in creating an exciting photo. The tension builds as we try to have all the elements perfect at the same time while the food is fresh under the camera. It's this creative tension and the anticipation of the result that are the most compelling aspects of any artistic endeavor and the reasons I return to the studio every day.

*Platter of Stuffed Shiitake Mushrooms, Spicy Scallop Salsa with
Ginger, Yakitori, and Thai Salmon Satay.*

CHAPTER 1

Win Sum and Dim Sum

Appetizers signal an evening of fun. The sight of pan-fried dumplings glazed with coconut-curry-basil sauce, the crunch of biting through a spring roll twice-fried to the ideal crispness, or the complex hoisin-garlic aroma of baby-back ribs drifting from the kitchen into the living room demands the collective attention of the group, intensifies the hunger, and forecasts coming culinary triumphs. But sight, sound, and aroma are only a hint of what all successful appetizers share: intense, complex flavors that fill the mouth with every bite. Pacific flavors offer so many alluring ways to achieve memorable taste memories. In this chapter we'll marinate cooked and chilled mussels with ginger, vinegar, and chiles before fitting them back into their shells. A side of salmon is cured with salt, Sichuan peppercorns, ginger, and vodka, then sliced paper thin and served with a spicy dipping sauce. In every recipe, it's the Pacific ingredients that create the intense, complex layering of flavors that makes everyone want to have another bite.

These appetizers can be served in many ways. For dinner, make only one Pacific-style appetizer, so that your guests arrive at the dining table filled with keen anticipation for the main course. Serve several appetizers as a quick, spectacular nibble before going out to dinner. Give an appetizer party, perhaps concluded by just a big garden salad and dessert. Or at a friend's no-host dinner, panfry Asian dumplings and watch as everyone gathers around the platter.

Thai Salmon Satay

12 bamboo skewers, 4 to
  6 inches long
1 pound skinless, center-cut
  salmon fillet
Pacific Flavors Dipping Sauces
  (pages 40–43) of your choice

SALMON-GRILLING MARINADE
3 tablespoons fresh lime juice
3 tablespoons flavorless
  cooking oil
3 tablespoons light brown sugar
2 tablespoons Thai or
  Vietnamese fish sauce
  or light soy sauce
1 teaspoon Asian chile sauce
2 tablespoons very finely
  minced ginger
3 tablespoons minced
  cilantro sprigs

At the Seafood Market Restaurant in Bangkok, tourists choose from 250 types of fresh and saltwater foods displayed at iced counters and then, through wild gestures and perhaps a few imperfectly spoken works of Thai, communicate to the chefs their choice of cooking technique and subtlety of seasoning. Customers sit at long tables and eat what only moments ago touched the searing sides of the wok. Iced Singha beer and crisp garlic bread mounded on plastic trays lessen but never entirely eliminate the eruption of flavor from Thai chiles. This is a tourist trap that is a great experience—at least for one evening.

ADVANCE PREPARATION

Soak the bamboo skewers in water for 1 to 6 hours. Cut the salmon into 12 rectangular pieces, each about 3 inches long, 1 inch wide, and ¼ inch thick. Push the skewer down the length of the salmon piece so that the skewer is visible only at either end. Repeat with remaining pieces, and refrigerate. Prepare chosen dipping sauce(s). Combine the marinade ingredients and refrigerate. *Can be completed up to 8 hours in advance of Last-Minute Cooking.*

LAST-MINUTE COOKING

Rub the marinade over the salmon and marinate for 15 minutes to 1 hour. If using a gas barbecue, heat to medium (350°F). If using charcoal or wood, prepare a fire. When the coals or wood are ash-covered, brush the barbecue rack with cooking oil and place salmon on rack. Grill the salmon for about 1 minute on each side. Brush with the reserved marinade during cooking.

To broil the salmon, place the broiling rack at the highest setting, then heat the broiler to 550°F. Line a baking sheet with foil, set a wire rack on top, and coat the rack with nonstick spray. Lay the salmon pieces on the rack and cover the exposed ends of the skewers with pieces of foil. Turn the oven setting to broil, and broil until the salmon loses its raw outside color, about 2 minutes. The skewers do not need to be turned while broiling. (If using an electric oven, leave the oven door slightly ajar during cooking.)

Serve at once, accompanied with one or more dipping sauces. Each person spoons a little of the sauce down the length of the salmon, and then nibbles the fish from around the skewer.

MENU IDEAS: Serve this with a substantial entrée, such as braised veal shanks.

Serves: 4 to 8 as an appetizer.

Yakitori

16 bamboo skewers, 4 to 6 inches
   long
4 chicken thighs, boned by your
   butcher
¾ cup Pacific Flavors Barbecue
   Sauce (page 105)
Peanut Satay Sauce (page 41)

Small fishing villages as well as the large cities of Japan offer a wealth of exciting food experiences for the traveler. Casual restaurants and food bars can be discerned by the red lanterns at the doors or by plastic replicas of their standard menu items displayed in front of the restaurants. We find it so much fun to eat rubata-yaki style. Seated at long counters and with rudimentary language skills, we point at our next course to be grilled by a smiling chef. Yakitori, *literally "grilled chicken," is a standard, succulent choice at these small restaurants. Use chicken thigh meat, which stays much more succulent than breast meat during barbecuing, and have your butcher complete the tedious boning of the thighs. Other types of meat that are good to barbecue on skewers are beef tenderloin, top sirloin, and meat from a leg of lamb.*

ADVANCE PREPARATION

Soak the bamboo skewers in water for 1 to 6 hours. Cut each thigh into 4 strips. Push a skewer down the length of each strip so that the skewer is visible only at either end of the chicken strip; refrigerate. Prepare the barbecue sauce. If cooking within 2 hours, rub over the chicken; otherwise, refrigerate marinade until ready to use. Prepare the satay sauce. *Can be completed to this point up to 8 hours in advance of Last-Minute Cooking.*

LAST-MINUTE COOKING

If using a gas barbecue, heat to medium (350°F). If using charcoal or wood, prepare a fire. When the coals or wood are ash-covered, brush the barbecue rack with cooking oil. Place the chicken strips on the rack over medium heat and grill for about 2 minutes on each side, basting with the marinade.

To broil the chicken, place the broiling rack at the highest setting, then heat the broiler to 550°F. Line a baking sheet with foil, set a wire rack on top, and coat the rack with nonstick spray. Lay the chicken strips on the rack and cover the exposed ends of the skewers with pieces of foil. Turn the oven setting to broil, and broil until the chicken is firm and has just lost its pink interior color, about 4 minutes (cut into a piece to make sure it is cooked). The skewers do not need to be turned while broiling.

Serve the chicken strips at once, accompanied with the dipping sauce. Each person spoons a little of the sauce down the length of the meat, and then nibbles the meat from around the skewer.

MENU IDEAS: As a dinner for four, serve with a Caesar salad, garlic bread, and fresh strawberries.

Serves: 4 to 8 as an appetizer.

Stuffed Shiitake Mushrooms

½ pound raw shrimp, shelled
   and deveined
½ of a large egg white
1 green onion, white and green
   parts, finely minced
2 teaspoons finely minced ginger
2 teaspoons light soy sauce
2 teaspoons Chinese rice wine
   or dry sherry
12 medium-size fresh shiitake
   mushrooms, stems removed
2 tablespoons flavorless
   cooking oil

SAUCE
¼ cup chicken stock
¼ cup coconut milk
2 tablespoons oyster sauce
1 teaspoon grated or finely
   minced lime zest
1 tablespoon fresh lime juice
½ teaspoon sugar
¼ teaspoons Asian chile sauce
2 tablespoons minced basil
   or cilantro sprigs

In this recipe, fresh shiitake mushrooms are stuffed with a seasoned shrimp mixture, panfried, and then cut into wedges as an appetizer. You can make this recipe with any size shiitake mushroom, but only buy shiitakes that are very fresh, with the edges of the caps curled and the gills still light brown and not wet. (Substituting twenty-four medium button mushrooms with the stems gently pulled off also works well.) We have tried other cooking methods, such as barbecuing, roasting, and broiling the stuffed mushrooms; however, if the heat is not perfect, the filling will not be fully cooked and the mushroom cap becomes too soft.

ADVANCE PREPARATION

In a bowl, mince the shrimp with the egg white. Add the green onion, ginger, soy sauce, and rice wine. Mix well. Fill the mushroom caps, pressing filling firmly into the caps; refrigerate. Set aside the cooking oil. Combine all the sauce ingredients, stir well, and refrigerate. *Can be completed to this point up to 8 hours in advance of Last-Minute Cooking.*

LAST-MINUTE COOKING

Place a 12- or 14-inch sauté pan over medium-high heat. Add the cooking oil, and when it becomes hot, add the mushrooms, stuffing side up. When the mushrooms begin to sizzle in the oil, pour the sauce around the sides of the pan. Cover the pan and steam the mushrooms until the filling turns white, about 1 minute. Immediately uncover the pan and continue cooking the mushrooms until all but ¼ cup of the sauce boils away, about 2 minutes. Transfer mushroom caps to a heated platter, and serve at once.

Serves: 4 to 8 as an appetizer.

Spicy Scallop Salsa with Ginger

1 head Bibb lettuce
$\frac{1}{4}$ cup pine nuts
2 tablespoons flavorless
    cooking oil
2 tablespoons very finely
    minced ginger
$\frac{1}{2}$ pound fresh bay scallops
3 medium vine-ripe tomatoes,
    seeded and chopped
$\frac{1}{2}$ hothouse cucumber, peeled
    and chopped into rough dice
1 green onion, white and green
    parts, minced
$\frac{1}{4}$ cup chopped cilantro sprigs
2 tablespoons fresh lime juice
2 tablespoons brown sugar
1 tablespoon Thai or
    Vietnamese fish sauce
2 teaspoons Asian chile sauce

This easy recipe has many variations. If fresh bay scallops are unavailable, substitute medium raw shrimp that are shelled, deveined, and butterflied. The scallops are sautéed only until they turn white on the outside, and thus are slightly undercooked in the center, but the shrimp must be sautéed until it turns white in the center (cut into one to see). Try replacing the tomato with one diced red bell pepper, or with cubed flesh of one slightly firm papaya or a perfectly ripe mango. If hothouse cucumbers are unavailable, use pickling cucumbers or the slender, rough-edged Japanese cucumbers. Regardless of the cucumber chosen, it is unnecessary to remove the peel.

ADVANCE PREPARATION

Separate the lettuce leaves, tearing any large leaves in half. Refrigerate the lettuce. Heat the oven to 325°F, and toast the pine nuts until light golden, about 8 minutes; transfer to a bowl and set aside. In a small bowl, combine the oil and ginger. Place a 12-inch sauté pan over high heat. When very hot, add the oil and ginger. Sauté for a few seconds, and then add the scallops. Stir and toss the scallops until they just turn white on the outside, about 30 seconds. Immediately transfer to a baking sheet. Spread the scallops into a single layer and refrigerate until thoroughly chilled.

In a bowl, combine all remaining ingredients. Mix well and refrigerate. *Can be completed to this point up to 5 hours in advance of serving.*

SERVING

Stir the salsa, adding the pine nuts. Taste and adjust the seasonings. Serve the salsa with the lettuce cups. Each person spoons a little salsa into a lettuce cup and eats the salsa-filled lettuce using the fingers.

Serves: 4 to 8 as an appetizer.

Sashimi Spring Rolls

½ pound fresh tuna,
    sashimi grade
½ pound raw shrimp
½ of a large egg white
2 small green onions, white
    and green parts, minced
2 tablespoons very finely
    minced ginger
2 teaspoons light soy sauce
¼ teaspoon sugar
24 large spinach leaves
12 spring roll skins
2 large eggs, well beaten
Pacific Flavors Dipping Sauces
    (page 40–43)
2 cups flavorless cooking oil

Steve Carey, executive chef at Leeann Chin's restaurant group, showed me how to make these striking-looking spring rolls. Across the paper-thin spring roll sheets are placed layers of spinach leaves, a finely minced shrimp filling, and strips of bright-red raw tuna. The spring rolls are then rolled into cylinders and given a brief, shallow frying. When the rolls are cut on a sharp diagonal, the still-raw tuna contrasts dramatically, both in color and flavor, with the white shrimp mixture and the emerald-green spinach. The key is to cook the spring rolls in very hot oil, which quickly turns them golden before the tuna has a chance to cook. However, if you are not sure that the shrimp has cooked, fry the spring rolls a little longer. Even if the tuna loses its raw color, the spring rolls will still taste delicious.

ADVANCE PREPARATION

Cut the tuna into twelve 4-inch-long strips. Shell and devein the shrimp, then, in a food processor, mince them finely with the egg white. In a bowl, combine the shrimp mixture, green onion, ginger, soy sauce, and sugar; mix thoroughly. Position a spring roll skin so that one of the corners is pointing at you. Lay 2 spinach leaves across the bottom third of the sheet. Spread about 2 tablespoons of the shrimp filling across the leaves. Add one strip of tuna. Roll the spinach leaves into a cylinder so the spinach encloses the filling. Bring the corner of the spring roll skin nearest you over the filling so that the two tips nearly meet. Roll the spring roll half a turn. Brush the sides with beaten egg. Fold each end over and then roll the spring roll into a cylinder. Cut away excess skin from the sides and top as you roll. Repeat with remaining filling and skins, transferring the spring rolls to a baking sheet in a single layer as you complete them. Refrigerate uncovered. Prepare one or more of the Pacific Flavors Dipping Sauces. *Can be completed to this point up to 8 hours in advance of Last-Minute Cooking.*

LAST-MINUTE COOKING

Place the cooking oil in a 12-inch sauté pan over medium-high heat, and heat to 375°. The oil must be hot enough so that the end of a bamboo chopstick will bubble when placed in the oil. Add half the spring rolls. Cook on all sides, and as soon as they turn a light golden, about 1 minute, drain on a wire rack. Cook the remaining spring rolls. Cut the spring rolls in half on the diagonal and transfer to a heated serving platter. Serve at once, accompanied by one or more dipping sauces.

Serves: 6 to 10 as an appetizer.

Goat Cheese with Pacific Flavors Rub

12 ounces soft goat cheese
2 tablespoons salted black beans
  (optional; see glossary)
3 cloves garlic, finely minced
2 tablespoons finely minced
  ginger
$\frac{1}{4}$ cup minced fresh mint
  leaves
$\frac{1}{4}$ cup minced cilantro sprigs
1 teaspoon finely minced or
  grated orange zest
2 teaspoons finely minced or
  grated lime zest
1 teaspoon Asian chile sauce
1 teaspoon sugar
$\frac{1}{2}$ cup flavorless cooking oil
2 teaspoons whole black
  peppercorns
2 teaspoons whole Sichuan
  peppercorns

This is one of the easiest recipes in the book. An oil infused with the flavors of peppers, garlic, ginger, and herbs is poured over thinly sliced goat cheese and then marinated for as short a time as four hours or as long as two days. As a variation, omit the black beans and chile sauce, or use any mix of basil leaves, mint, and cilantro for the fresh herbs.

ADVANCE PREPARATION

Cut the goat cheese crosswise into $\frac{1}{2}$-inch pieces, and place in a single layer in a ceramic container. Rinse and chop the black beans, if using, and combine with the garlic, ginger, mint, and cilantro in a small bowl. In a separate bowl, combine the grated orange and lime zests, chile sauce, and sugar.

Place the oil in a 10-inch sauté pan over medium-high heat. Add the peppercorns. When peppercorns begin to "pop," remove the pan from the heat and immediately stir in the garlic mixture. After 15 seconds, stir in the chile sauce mixture. Immediately pour the infused oil over the goat cheese and refrigerate for at least 4 hours. Turn the goat cheese over at least once, spooning the oil over the top. *Can be completed to this point up to two days in advance of serving.*

SERVING

Transfer the goat cheese to a platter. Bring to room temperature, and accompany with crackers.

Serves: 8 to 12 as an appetizer.

Spicy Marinated Mussels

Spicy Marinated Mussels

TO STEAM MUSSELS
18 small mussels
Salt

MARINADE
1/4 cup slivered red bell pepper
2 tablespoons chopped
  cilantro sprigs
2 tablespoons minced green
  onion, green and white parts
1 clove garlic, finely minced
1 tablespoon finely minced
  ginger
3 tablespoons white-wine
  vinegar
2 tablespoons dark sesame oil
1 tablespoon safflower oil
1/2 teaspoon Asian chile sauce
1/4 teaspoon salt

TO FINISH
3 tablespoons olive oil
  (not extra-virgin)

Chilled mussels tossed with a spicy herb-flavored dressing make a dramatic beginning to a dinner. Since the easy preparation steps can be completed hours in advance, all you need to do when your friends arrive is bring the platter holding the mussels from the refrigerator to the living room. But mussels do require careful storing and cleaning. Only buy mussels that are tightly closed, which indicates that they are still alive and thus at the very peak of freshness. To store mussels, transfer them to a colander or sieve placed in a larger bowl. Cover the mussels with a kitchen towel saturated with cold water, add a few ice cubes, and refrigerate. Stored in this manner, the mussels will be able to breath and stay fresh for 24 hours. When you begin preparing this dish, place all the mussels in a bowl, cover with cold water, and give a few vigorous stirs using your hands. Discard any mussels that are not tightly closed, as this indicates that the mussels have perished before you had the opportunity to cook them! Because of this attrition, it's a good idea to buy a few extra mussels just in case you have to discard a few. For non-mussel lovers, toss 1 1/2 pounds of cooked, chilled shrimp that have been shelled and deveined with the marinade and serve at once.

ADVANCE PREPARATION

Scrub the mussels vigorously, pulling away the beards and any seaweed from between the shells. In a 4-quart pot, bring 1 inch of water to a vigorous boil. Lightly salt the water, then add the mussels and cover the pot. Cook until the mussels open, about 3 minutes. Transfer to a colander, let cool, then refrigerate for 1 hour. Discard any mussels that did not open.

Combine the ingredients for the marinade and mix well. Carefully remove the mussel meat, saving the shells, and toss meat with the marinade. Open the mussel shells wide, but do not detach the halves. Place the shells in a bowl, add the olive oil, and gently toss until evenly coated. Transfer the shells to a plate and place a marinated mussel in each shell. Refrigerate until ready to serve. *Can be completed to this point up to 8 hours in advance of serving.*

To serve, place the mussels on a decorative plate.

MENU IDEAS—Dinner for four: Spicy Marinated Mussels, Smoked Baby Back Ribs with Pacific Flavors Barbecue Sauce (page 105), a tossed green salad with California Cornbread (page 151), and homemade ice cream.

Serves: 4 to 8 as an appetizer or 4 as a first course.

Ginger Gravlax

½ pound fresh salmon fillet,
    skin and pin bones removed
    by fishmonger

MARINADE
¼ cup minced ginger
¼ cup chopped cilantro sprigs
¼ cup vodka
2 tablespoons light soy sauce
1 tablespoon sugar
1 tablespoon salt
1 tablespoon crushed Sichuan
    peppercorns
1 teaspoon Asian chile sauce

Ginger Mustard Sauce (page 42)
    or another sauce from pages
    40–43
Cilantro sprigs
Thin baguette, about 1 foot long
4 tablespoons (½ stick)
    unsalted butter, at room
    temperature

Salmon marinated in ginger, Sichuan peppercorns, and vodka results in a blossoming of flavors. These little pyramids alternate colors and tastes, starting with thinly sliced and toasted baguettes, then a ribbon of gravlax, a drizzle of Ginger Mustard Sauce, and sprigs of cilantro as crowns. As an alternative, let guests assemble their own appetizer, choosing from various crackers and thinly sliced breads, then topping the paper-thin salmon slices with one of several Pacific Flavors Dipping Sauces and fresh herb sprigs. Leftover gravlax makes an excellent lunch or dinner entrée thinly sliced and included in a green salad tossed with an oil-and-vinegar dressing. In terms of recipe planning, the salmon needs to marinate for a minimum of two days.

ADVANCE PREPARATION

Check salmon for stray bones and remove. Combine the marinade ingredients. Place salmon and marinade in a small plastic food bag. Seal, put on a tray, and place in the refrigerator. Then place a 5-quart pot filled with cold water on top of the salmon. Refrigerate for 2 to 3 days. It is unnecessary to turn the salmon. *Recipe must be prepared up to this point 2 to 3 days in advance of Last-Minute Preparation.*

LAST-MINUTE COOKING

The day you plant to serve the dish, have the Ginger Mustard Sauce or another sauce ready. Set aside the cilantro. Cut the baguette crosswise into 24 very thin pieces. Toast lightly on both sides under the broiler, then lightly butter one side.

    With a wet hand, wipe the marinade off the salmon on both sides. Very thinly slice the salmon, keeping the blade wet so the fish does not tear. Press plastic wrap across the pieces so that the slices do not dry out, and refrigerate until ready to serve. You should have about 24 pieces. Just before serving, place a slice of salmon on each piece of bread, add a little drizzle of sauce, and garnish with a cilantro sprig. Serve at once.

Serves: 6 to 8 as an appetizer.

Chile Shrimp with Basil

1 pound medium to large raw
  shrimp
½ red bell pepper
8 chives
2 tablespoons unsalted roasted
  peanuts (optional)

SAUCE
2 tablespoons Thai or
  Vietnamese fish sauce or
  light soy sauce
2 tablespoons fresh lime juice
2 tablespoons light brown sugar
2 tablespoons flavorless
  cooking oil
1 teaspoon Asian chile sauce
1 tablespoon very finely minced
  ginger
2 cloves garlic, finely minced
¼ cup chopped fresh basil
  leaves or cilantro sprigs

No matter how we plan to use shrimp, we always buy large ones that have a per-pound count of about sixteen pieces. While they are more expensive than smaller shrimp, they are much easier to shell and devein, and make a dramatic presentation. In terms of technique, it's important to remember that even large shrimp cook very quickly in boiling water—about thirty to sixty seconds. Once you have stirred the shrimp into the boiling water, the moment all the shrimp turn white remove a shrimp and cut into it. If it's still translucent in the center, return the shrimp, cook another ten seconds, and then remove another shrimp to test again. The moment you cut into a shrimp and it is white in the center, tip all the shrimp into a colander and immediately transfer to a large bowl filled with ice and cold water. That's how to achieve perfectly cooked shrimp every time.

ADVANCE PREPARATION

Shell the shrimp, then cut each one deeply along the top and rinse out the vein. Bring 4 quarts of water to a rapid boil and add the shrimp. Cook until shrimp are done, about 1 minute. To test, cut a shrimp in half; it should be white in the center. Immediately drain the shrimp in a colander, and then transfer to a bowl of ice water to cool. When chilled, drain and refrigerate until ready to use.

Mince and place in separate containers the red pepper and chives. Finely chop the peanuts in a food processor and set aside. Combine the sauce ingredients and mix well. *Can be completed to this point up to 10 hours in advance of Last-Minute Preparation.*

LAST-MINUTE PREPARATION

Toss the shrimp with the sauce. Put in a decorative bowl and place the bowl in crushed ice. Sprinkle the shrimp with the red pepper, chives, and peanuts. Serve at once.

Serves: 4 to 8 as an appetizer or 4 as a first course.

Firecracker Dumplings and Crisp Spring Rolls (recipe on page 28)

Firecracker Dumplings

This is one of our favorite dumpling recipes. The filling can be made quickly and the dumplings folded and then refrigerated or frozen. The cooking process is just as easy, for the dumplings are cooked in boiling water before being tossed in a rich Chinese "pesto" sauce. Firecracker Dumplings are excellent as an hors d'oeuvre or entrée accompanied by the same dishes you might have when serving homemade ravioli.

¹⁄₄ cup cornstarch, for dusting
2 green onions, white and green parts
1 pound ground raw veal, pork, or chicken
1 tablespoon oyster sauce
2 teaspoons Chinese rice wine or dry sherry
1 teaspoon dark sesame oil
1 teaspoon Asian chile sauce
1 large egg
1 tablespoon white sesame seeds
30 wonton skins or round gyoza skins

DRESSING
2 cups spinach leaves, washed and dried

¹⁄₄ cup cilantro sprigs
8 basil leaves
1 green onion, white and green parts, chopped
2 cloves garlic, chopped
2 teaspoons minced ginger
1 teaspoon grated or minced orange peel
1 tablespoon light soy sauce
2 tablespoons Chinese rice wine or dry sherry
2 tablespoons distilled white vinegar
2 tablespoons dark sesame oil
2 teaspoons hoisin sauce
2 teaspoons sugar
¹⁄₂ teaspoon Asian chile sauce

ADVANCE PREPARATION

Line a baking sheet with parchment paper and dust with cornstarch. Set aside. Mince the green onions in a food processor. Transfer to a bowl and add the ground meat, oyster sauce, rice wine or sherry, sesame oil, chile sauce, and egg. Thoroughly mix and set aside. Toast the sesame seeds until golden in an ungreased skillet, then set aside. Within 5 hours of cooking, assemble the dumplings. Trim the wontons into circles, then place 2 teaspoons of filling in the center of each one. Moisten the edges with water and fold the dumpling in half over the filling, being careful not to flatten the filling. Press the edges of each wonton together; the dumplings will be a half-moon shape. Moisten one end of the dumpling, then pinch the ends together. The dumpling should now look like a little cap. Place on the baking sheet and refrigerate, uncovered.

To prepare the dressing, place all the ingredients in a blender and liquefy. Transfer to a small bowl and refrigerate. *Can be completed to this point up to 12 hours in advance of Last-Minute Cooking.*

(recipe continues on next page)

LAST-MINUTE COOKING

Bring 5 quarts of water to a vigorous boil. Add the dumplings and give them a gentle stir. When all the dumplings float to the surface (about 3 minutes), gently tip into a colander and drain thoroughly. Transfer the dumplings to a mixing bowl. Add the dressing and toss. Transfer the dumplings to a heated serving platter, sprinkle on the sesame seeds, and serve at once.

MENU IDEAS: A menu with a vegetarian emphasis—Firecracker Dumplings, Stir-Fried Garden Vegetables (page 134) served with steamed jasmine rice, Crazy Caesar Salad (page 63), and fresh fruit.

Serves: 6 to 8 as an appetizer, or 4 as an entrée.

Crisp Spring Rolls with Lettuce and Mint Wrap

4 cups spinach leaves, washed and stemmed
3/4 pound raw shrimp, shelled, deveined, and finely minced
1/4 pound fresh lump crabmeat (optional), picked over
2 green onions, white and green parts, minced
2 tablespoons finely minced ginger
1 tablespoon finely minced or grated lemon skin
1 tablespoon oyster sauce
1/2 teaspoon Asian chile sauce
12 spring roll skins
2 large eggs, well beaten
One or more Pacific Flavors Dipping Sauces (pages 40-43)
1 head Bibb lettuce
1 bunch fresh mint
2 cups flavorless cooking oil

Chinese spring rolls are traditionally filled with a mixture of shredded pork, cabbage, bamboo shoots, and bean sprouts that has been stir-fried and then thoroughly chilled before being wrapped in spring roll skins. This recipe provides a far easier method and just as tasty a result. Spring roll skins are cut in half corner to corner, and then filled with a raw dim sum filling. Because the skins have been cut in half, the small amount of filling cooks quickly during the shallow-frying process. For a variation, substitute any of the dumpling fillings in this chapter.

ADVANCE PREPARATION

Bring an inch of water to a boil in a 2-quart saucepan, add the spinach, and cook, stirring, just until it wilts, about 10 seconds; immediately transfer to a sieve, rinse with cold water, and then press all the moisture from the spinach. Mince; combine with the shrimp, crabmeat, if using, green onions, oyster sauce, and chile sauce in a large bowl; mix well.

Cut the spring roll skins in half diagonally. Position a skin so the long side is facing you. Place about 1/2 cup of the filling along the bottom third of the skin, forming the filling into a long cylinder. Fold the left-hand corner over the filling and brush surface with beaten egg. Fold the right-hand corner over, pressing to seal. Brush surface with egg, then gently roll. Seal the top corner with a little more egg. Repeat with remaining filling and skins. Transfer to a baking sheet in a single layer, and refrigerate uncovered.

Prepare one or more of the dipping sauces. Separate the lettuce leaves, discard any thick stems, and refrigerate the lettuce. Separate mint leaves from their stems, and refrigerate the leaves. *Can be completed to this point up to 8 hours in advance of Last-Minute Cooking.*

LAST-MINUTE COOKING

Pour the oil into a 12-inch sauté pan. Place over high heat, and heat the oil until the tip of a wooden chopstick bubbles when placed in the oil. Fry half the spring rolls, cooking them on all sides until they turn a very light golden brown, then drain on a wire rack. Cook the rest of the spring rolls.

Heat the oil again until it becomes very hot, about 400°F, but not so hot that it begins to smoke. Return half the spring rolls to the oil, and fry until they become dark golden brown, about 30 seconds. Drain. Repeat with the remaining spring rolls.

Transfer the spring rolls to a heated platter and accompany with dipping sauces, lettuce leaves, and mint. Each person wraps a spring roll and mint leaf in a lettuce leaf, dips the end into a dipping sauce, and eats using the fingers.

Serves: 8 to 12 as an appetizer.

Scallop Ravioli in Saffron-Caviar Sauce

¼ cup cornstarch, for dusting
4 cups spinach leaves
1 green onion, white and green parts
½ pound fresh bay scallops
¼ pound ground raw veal, pork, or chicken
1 tablespoon finely minced ginger
1 tablespoon oyster sauce
2 teaspoons Chinese rice wine or dry sherry
30 wonton skins or round gyoza skins

GARNISH
2 ounces top-quality black caviar
¼ cup Asian chile sauce
1 bunch chives

SAUCE
2 cups heavy cream
½ cup Chinese rice wine or dry sherry
2 teaspoons dark sesame oil
½ teaspoon salt
Pinch of saffron threads
1½ tablespoons finely minced ginger

A dish we tasted at Michel Richard's quintessentially California restaurant, Citrus, inspired these dumplings. The tender scallop dumplings, glazed with a rich ginger-cream sauce, are accented by Asian chile sauce and caviar. A New Year's Eve appetizer party for ten might include this recipe plus Ginger Gravlax, Yakitori with Peanut Satay Sauce, and chilled vegetables with two Pacific Flavors Dipping Sauces. Accompanied by Dom Perignon Champagne, this would be a glorious way to anticipate the new year!

ADVANCE PREPARATION

Line a baking sheet with parchment paper and dust with cornstarch. Set aside. Drop the spinach leaves into an inch of boiling water. Stir the spinach, and when it wilts (about 10 seconds), transfer to a colander and rinse under cold water. Using your hands, press all the moisture from the leaves. Mince the spinach, green onion, and scallops separately. Transfer to a bowl and add ground meat, ginger, oyster sauce, and rice wine or sherry. Mix thoroughly. Within 5 hours of cooking, assemble the ravioli. If using wontons, trim into circles. Follow the folding instructions given on page 27, folding the dumplings into either half-moon shapes or into caps. Place on the baking sheet and refrigerate, uncovered.

Separately set aside the caviar and chile sauce. Mince the chives and set aside. In a small bowl, combine the sauce ingredients. *Can be completed to this point up to 12 hours in advance of Last-Minute Cooking.*

LAST-MINUTE COOKING

Pour the sauce into a 12-inch skillet. Bring to a vigorous boil over high heat and cook until the sauce thickens enough so the spoon leaves a "path" as the sauce is stirred, about 8 minutes. Turn the heat to very low and keep warm.

Bring 5 quarts of water to a vigorous boil. Add the ravioli and give them a gentle stir. When the ravioli float to the surface (about 3 minutes), gently tip them into a colander to drain. Transfer the ravioli to serving plates. Spoon the sauce over the top. Sprinkle on the chopped chives, then decorate each plate with a little caviar and dots of chile sauce. Serve at once.

Serves: 4 to 8 as an hors d'oeuvre or first course or 2 as an entrée.

Tex-Mex Wontons with New Age Guacamole

2 green onions, white and
   green parts
1 ear white sweet corn
2 cloves garlic, finely minced
½ pound ground lamb
1 tablespoon oyster sauce
1 tablespoon light soy sauce
½ large egg, well beaten
1 teaspoon Asian chile sauce
¼ cup cornstarch, for dusting

TO ASSEMBLE
24 wonton skins
New Age Guacamole (page 42)
Flavorless cooking oil, for
   shallow frying

Whenever possible, we try to serve food that creates a surprise, and this recipe is a perfect example. The traditional Chinese pork filling is replaced with a lamb-and-corn filling accented by garlic-and-chile sauce. With each bite through the crisp skin, the corn adds crunch and releases its sweetness, while the lamb has more depth of flavor than pork. Dipped into a buttery guacamole rather than into a predictable Chinese sweet-and-sour sauce, all the texture and flavor elements make such an exciting match that it is impossible to serve enough of these wontons to satisfy a gathering of friends.

ADVANCE PREPARATION

Mince the green onions in a food professor. Transfer to a mixing bowl. Stand the ear of corn on one end and cut off all the kernels. Add the raw kernels to the bowl along with the garlic, lamb, oyster and soy sauces, beaten egg, and chile sauce. Mix thoroughly. Line a baking sheet with parchment paper and dust with cornstarch. Set aside.

Assemble the dumplings: With one point of a wonton skin facing you, place 1½ teaspoons of filling in the center. Fold the skin in half by bringing the opposite tip forward over the filling; the wonton tips should not quite meet each other. Roll the wonton once into a cylinder with the side tips still open. Turn the cylinder 180° and lightly moisten each end of the cylinder with water. Touch the moistened tips together, forming a cap. Place wontons on the baking sheet and refrigerate, uncovered. Prepare the guacamole. *Can be completed to this point up to 12 hours in advance of Last-Minute Cooking.*

LAST-MINUTE COOKING

In a 12-inch skillet, heat ½ inch of cooking oil to 365°F. To test the oil, drop in a little piece of wonton skin; if the oil is hot enough, the skin will bounce across the surface. Add about 10 wontons to the oil and fry until golden on one side, then turn and fry on the other side, about 1½ minutes total. Drain the wontons on a wire rack while you fry the remainder. Serve with New Age Guacamole.

MENU IDEAS: A New Age dinner for eight—Tex-Mex Wontons with New Age Guacamole, a baby greens salad tossed with an oil-and-vinegar dressing, Thai Sautéed Shrimp (page 86) served with rice pilaf, and Lemon Ice Cream with Chocolate Grand Marnier Sauce (page 159). Accompany with imported beers and iced herb teas.

Serves: 6 to 12 as an appetizer.

Tex-Mex Wontons with New Age Guacamole

Thai Shrimp Pizza

CRUST
1½ teaspoons active dry yeast
2 teaspoons sugar
¾ cup warm water
  (105°–115°F)
2 tablespoons olive oil
1½ teaspoons salt
¼ cup minced fresh basil leaves
2 cups bread flour

TOPPING
2 tablespoons olive oil
1 large clove garlic, very finely
  minced
1 pound raw medium shrimp
2 tablespoons fresh lime juice
2 tablespoons fish sauce
1 tablespoon honey
4 ounces part-skim mozzarella
  cheese, grated
¼ cup finely chopped unsalted
  roasted peanuts
⅓ cup chopped fresh mint
  leaves or cilantro sprigs
2 teaspoons grated or minced
  lime zest

¼ cup cornmeal, for paddle

Pizzas make great appetizers. The dough can be made hours in advance and kept in the refrigerator along with all the toppings. We like to enlist the aid of guests to help roll out the dough, scatter on the toppings, and monitor the baking. The moment the pizzas come out of the oven, there is always a collective gasp of eager anticipation. In terms of technique, the key to great homemade pizzas is using a pizza stone. Only a pizza stone can vaporize the dough's moisture and create a truly crisp skin. Pizza stones are sold by all cookware and most hardware stores. Purchase the thickest and biggest one, along with a wooden pizza paddle. Now you will be able to transfer the pizza in and out of the oven like a professional!

ADVANCE PREPARATION

Prepare the dough: Sprinkle the yeast and sugar over the warm water. When bubbles appear on top (about 5 minutes), stir in the olive oil, salt, and basil. Stir the yeast mixture into the flour. Lightly flour your hands and knead the dough until smooth and no longer sticky, about 5 minutes. Lightly oil a small bowl. Rotate the dough in the bowl to coat with oil, cover with a towel, and let rise for about 45 minutes in a warm area of the kitchen. Knead briefly again, cover, and let rise for another 30 minutes. If not using immediately, refrigerate.

Prepare the topping: Combine the oil and garlic. Shell, devein, and split the shrimp in half; refrigerate. In a small bowl, combine the lime juice, fish sauce, and honey; refrigerate. Refrigerate the cheese; separately set aside the mint, grated lime, and peanuts. *Can be completed to this point up to 8 hours in advance of Last-Minute Cooking.*

LAST-MINUTE COOKING

Have the herbs and zest ready. Place a pizza stone on the lowest oven rack, heat the oven to 550°, and wait 30 minutes, until the stone becomes evenly heated. Combine the shrimp with the lime-juice mixture. On a lightly floured surface, roll out the dough into a 12- to 18-inch round. Rub the oil and garlic over the top. Transfer the dough to a pizza paddle sprinkled with cornmeal. Drain the shrimp and scatter them evenly over the dough. Sprinkle on the cheese and half the mint. Slide the pizza onto the stone and cook until the edges are golden, about 8 minutes. Using the paddle, remove the pizza from the oven. Sprinkle the pizza with remaining mint, grated lime, and peanuts. Cut into wedges; serve at once.

MENU IDEAS—Pacific Flavors appetizer party for twelve around the pool: Thai Shrimp Pizza, Yakitori (page 17), Goat Cheese with Pacific Flavors Rub (page 21), and Spicy Marinated Mussels (page 23).

Serves: 6 to 12 as an appetizer or 6 as a first course.

Wok-Seared Beef in Endive Cups

½ pound beef tenderloin,
   trimmed of all fat
1 tablespoon hoisin sauce
1 tablespoon oyster sauce
1 tablespoon dark sesame oil
1 tablespoon Chinese rice wine
   or dry sherry
1 teaspoon Asian chile sauce
3 cloves garlic, finely minced
2 green onions, white and green
   parts, shredded
¼ cup mint leaves
20 large endive leaves (about 2
   heads)
2 tablespoons flavorless
   cooking oil

Stir-frys make great appetizers. The preparation can be completed hours in advance, and the last-minute cooking takes only seconds. Any stir-fry recipe can be converted into an appetizer: Just dice or matchstick-cut the main ingredients so they will easily fit into an endive leaf or other type of lettuce cup. Complete the cooking after all the guests arrive, perhaps enlisting a friend to help position the stir-fry on a platter and to place the endive cups around the outside edges. Follow the stir-fry appetizer with dinner selections that require no last-minute cooking.

ADVANCE PREPARATION

Cut the meat across the grain in the thinnest possible slices. Overlap the slices and cut into ¼-inch-wide matchsticks. Transfer the meat to a bowl, and add hoisin and oyster sauces, sesame oil, rice wine or sherry, chile sauce, and garlic. Mix thoroughly and refrigerate. Shred green onions and mint leaves; combine and refrigerate. Set aside endive cups. *Can be completed to this point up to 8 hours in advance of Last-Minute Cooking.*

LAST-MINUTE COOKING

Place the wok over highest heat. When the wok becomes very hot, add the cooking oil. Roll the oil around the sides of the wok. As soon as the oil begins to smoke, add the beef and marinade. Stir and toss the beef, separating all the pieces, and cook until all the beef just loses its raw outside color. Add the green onions and mint. Stir-fry another 15 seconds.

    Slide the stir-fry onto a platter. Ring the platter with endive cups. Serve at once. Each person spoons a little of the filling into an endive cup, and eats the cup using the fingers.

MENU IDEAS: As a dinner for six, Endive with Wok-Seared Beef in Endive Cups, Sichuan Veal Meat Loaf (page 98) with sourdough rolls, Crazy Caesar Salad (page 63), and a hot peach pie.

Serves: 6 to 12 as an appetizer or 6 as a first course.

Thai Fried Dumplings

¼ cup cornstarch, for dusting
4 cups spinach leaves
2 small green onions, white and green parts
¾ pound raw shrimp, shelled and deveined
1 tablespoon finely minced fresh ginger
1 tablespoon oyster soy sauce
¼ teaspoon Asian chile sauce
24 wonton skins or round gyoza skins
2 tablespoons flavorless cooking oil

SAUCE
1 tablespoon minced fresh basil leaves
1 tablespoon minced fresh mint leaves
1 tablespoon minced green onion, white and green parts
¼ cup unsweetened coconut milk
¼ cup chicken broth, preferably homemade (page 69)
2 tablespoons Chinese rice wine or dry sherry
1 tablespoon oyster sauce
½ tablespoon curry powder
½ teaspoon sugar

Dumplings filled with seafood or meat and browned in a frying pan until the bottoms turn a deep golden always appear as an appetizer at our parties. As guests crunch through the crisp skins, each bite reveals a savory filling accented by a rich sauce. We always complete the preparation hours in advance and then enlist the aid of our guests to help fold the dumplings. This little aerobic activity begins the evening in a relaxed fashion and we are spared the much longer time it takes to fold the dumplings alone.

ADVANCE PREPARATION

Line a baking sheet with parchment paper and dust with cornstarch. Set aside. Blanch and mince the spinach as described on page 30. In a food processor, separately mince the green onions and shrimp. In a bowl, combine the spinach, onions, shrimp, ginger, oyster sauce, and chile sauce. Mix thoroughly and refrigerate. Within 12 hours of cooking, assemble the dumplings. Trim the wontons into circles. Place 1 tablespoon of the filling on the center of each wonton skin. Bring the edges of the skin up around the filling. Wrap your thumb and index finger around its "waist" and squeeze, at the same time pressing the top and bottom of the dumpling with your other index finger and thumb. The dumplings should look like cylinders with flat tops and bottoms. Place the dumplings on the baking sheet; refrigerate. Combine the sauce ingredients and refrigerate. *Can be completed to this point up to 12 hours in advance of Last-Minute Cooking.*

LAST-MINUTE COOKING

Place a 12-inch nonstick skillet over high heat. Add the cooking oil and immediately add dumplings, flat bottom down. Fry the dumplings until the bottoms are dark golden, about 2 minutes. Pour in the sauce and immediately cover pan. Cook dumplings until they are firm to the touch, about 1 minute. Remove cover and increase heat to high. Continue frying dumplings until the sauce reduces completely, about 30 seconds. While cooking, shake the pan so that the dumplings are glazed all over with the sauce. Tip out onto a heated serving platter and serve at once.

MENU IDEAS: Pacific Flavors dinner for four—Thai Fried Dumplings, Asian Roasted Red Pepper Salad (page 50), and Warm Chocolate Crème Brûlée (page 162).

Serves: 4 to 8 as an hors d'oeuvre or first course, or 2 as an entrée.

Asian Summer Rolls

½ pound medium raw shrimp, shelled and deveined
2 cups shredded iceberg lettuce
12 cilantro sprigs
12 fresh mint leaves
¼ cup chopped roasted peanuts, unsalted
12 rice-paper rounds, 6½ inches in diameter
One or more Pacific Flavors Dipping Sauces, page 40–43

This recipe uses Vietnamese rice paper, which is paper-thin sheets of transparent rice "paper" made from rice flour, and sold at room temperature. Filled with herbs, shrimp, and lettuce, these summer rolls are served uncooked and accompanied by various dipping sauces. Try varying the filling by substituting fresh lump crabmeat in place of the shrimp, or experimenting with different lettuces and toasted nuts. Since learning how to handle the rice paper takes a little trial and error, make these in the morning so you have plenty of time to perfect the process. In terms of technique, if the rice paper is moistened with too much water, it will disintegrate; if it is too dry, the rice paper will crack as it is rolled into a cylinder. If you have trouble with sheets breaking, lay a second sheet on top.

ADVANCE PREPARATION

Bring 2 quarts of water to a boil; stir in the shrimp. As soon as they turn white in the center, about 30 seconds (cut into a shrimp to test), tip into a colander and transfer immediately to a bowl holding a generous amount of iced water. When chilled, pat dry. Set aside the lettuce, cilantro, mint, and peanuts separately.

Dip a piece of rice paper in hot water. Place a shrimp about ½ inch from the bottom edge (along the long side). Add a small amount of lettuce, one cilantro sprig, one mint leaf, and a sprinkling of nuts. Fold each side over, and roll the rice paper tightly into a cylinder. Repeat with remaining ingredients and rice paper. Transfer cylinders to a baking sheet in a single layer, cover with plastic wrap and a damp dish towel, then refrigerate. Prepare one or more of the dipping sauces. *Can be completed to this point up to 8 hours in advance of serving.*

SERVING

Transfer the rice-paper rolls to a serving platter. Serve accompanied by dipping sauces.

Serves: 4 to 8 as an appetizer.

PACIFIC FLAVORS DIPPING SAUCES

The appealing aspect of dipping sauces is that they add a special taste to many dishes, particularly appetizers. Use these sauces for chilled cooked shrimp and other seafood, as dips for vegetables, to glaze crisp deep-fried wontons and spring rolls, for drizzling over ribbons of barbecued meat and seafood placed on skewers, and for rubbing across the surface of Peking Chive Pancakes or tortillas before adding a filling of barbecued meat and lettuce. Pacific Flavors Dipping Sauces are great with crisp tortilla chips, or to plunge shrimp into as they arrive sizzling hot, straight from the wok or grill. Use these recipes as a starting point for creating your own variations.

Plum Lemon Dip

1 tablespoon white sesame seeds	2 tablespoons fresh lemon juice
$1/4$ teaspoon finely minced garlic	5 tablespoons plum sauce
$1/2$ teaspoon grated or finely minced lemon zest	$1/4$ teaspoon Asian chile sauce
	$1/8$ teaspoon ground cinnamon

ADVANCE PREPARATION

Toast the sesame seeds in a small skillet until golden, about 4 minutes. Combine with the remaining ingredients, then refrigerate. Use within 3 weeks. *Makes $1/2$ cup.*

Apricot Sweet and Sour Sauce

This is one of our favorite and most versatile dipping sauces. We especially like to combine ¹/₄ cup of the apricot sauce with a light-grade olive oil and rice vinegar to create an apricot vinaigrette.

15 dried apricots
12 ounces apricot nectar (sold in the juice section of most supermarkets)
¹/₂ cup water

¹/₂ cup sugar
¹/₂ cup distilled white vinegar
1 teaspoon Asian chile sauce
1 tablespoon minced ginger

ADVANCE PREPARATION

Place all the ingredients in a nonreactive saucepan over medium-high heat. Bring to a low boil, reduce the heat to low, cover, and simmer for 25 minutes. Transfer to a blender and blend thoroughly, about 30 seconds. Cool and refrigerate. Use within 3 weeks. *Makes 3 cups.*

Peanut Satay Sauce

Great peanut sauces depend on using great peanut butter. For this recipe always buy "natural" or "organic" peanut butter, the only ingredients of which are salt and roasted peanuts. The sauce will last indefinitely refrigerated provided that the green onions are omitted. Make it in larger amounts, and add the minced green onions just to the portion you use that day.

¹/₂ cup chunky salted peanut butter
¹/₄ cup Chinese rice wine or dry sherry
2 tablespoons honey
2 tablespoons white-wine vinegar
2 tablespoons flavorless cooking oil
1 tablespoons dark sesame oil
1 tablespoon dark soy sauce

1 teaspoon Asian chile sauce
2 cloves garlic, finely minced
2 tablespoons very finely minced ginger
2 tablespoons finely minced green onion, white and green parts

ADVANCE PREPARATION

Combine all the ingredients. Stir well. Depending on the type of peanut butter used, you may need to thin the dipping sauce by stirring in a little cold water. Store in the refrigerator. *Makes 1¹/₄ cups.*

Ginger Mustard Sauce

Little dots of Ginger Mustard Sauce make a great flavor accent for chilled cooked fish and shrimp, and with deep-fried wontons and spring rolls.

3 tablespoons very finely minced ginger
3–4 tablespoons dry mustard
¼ cup beer
1 tablespoon honey

2 tablespoons Dijon mustard
2 tablespoons Japanese rice vinegar, unseasoned
¼ teaspoon salt

ADVANCE PREPARATION

Combine all the ingredients. Transfer to a bowl and refrigerate. Use within 2 weeks. *Makes 1 cup.*

New Age Guacamole

It's great to create surprise when serving food. Here the surprises are sweet corn kernels and chopped fresh water chestnuts, which add extra color, texture, and flavor. To retain the bright green of freshly made guacamole during hours of storage, add a paper-thin film of milk across the surface. Don't use lactose-free milk, because it's the lactic acid that prevents discoloration. Any type of milk, from non-fat to regular milk, that has lactic acid will work. Just before using, stir the guacamole to incorporate the milk. The milk will not discolor the guacamole or add any flavor.

¾ cup mashed ripe avocado (about 1 medium)
½ cup chopped fresh water chestnuts or jicama
1 ear white corn, husked
2 tablespoons minced green onions, white and green parts

1 tablespoon minced cilantro sprigs
½ teaspoon finely minced garlic
1 tablespoon fresh lemon juice, or to taste
1 teaspoon Asian chile sauce
¼ teaspoon salt
1 tablespoon milk, optional

ADVANCE PREPARATION

In a mixing bowl, combine the avocado and water chestnuts or jicama. Standing the corn on one end, cut off all the kernels. Add the kernels to the avocado along with the remaining ingredients. Mix thoroughly. If doing this in advance, transfer to a small bowl, press the guacamole to firmly pack it, smooth the surface, and cover the surface with a tablespoon of milk. Press plastic wrap onto the surface of the guacamole and refrigerate for up to 12 hours. To use, stir the guacamole and serve. *Makes 1½ cups.*

Thai Dipping Sauce

Variations of this sweet, sour, spicy dipping sauce are served throughout Southeast Asia. Because the flavor of fresh lime juice deteriorates quickly, use this dipping sauce the day it is made.

2¹/₂ tablespoons water
2 tablespoons Thai or Vietnamese
  fish sauce
2 tablespoons fresh lime juice
2 teaspoons honey

¹/₂ teaspoon Asian chile sauce
1 clove garlic, finely minced
1 tablespoon shredded fresh basil
  or mint leaves
2 teaspoons shredded ginger

ADVANCE PREPARATION

Combine all the ingredients. Taste and adjust the flavors depending on your preference for sourness, sweetness, and spiciness. Serve at room temperature and use the same day. *Makes ¹/₂ cup.*

Thai Red Curry Dip

2 dried ancho chiles
3 medium vine-ripened tomatoes,
  stemmed and seeded
1 small shallot
4 cloves garlic
¹/₄ cup white-wine vinegar

2 tablespoons sugar
2 tablespoons Thai or Vietnamese
  fish sauce
1 teaspoon ground coriander
1 teaspoon Asian chile sauce

ADVANCE PREPARATION

Cover ancho chiles with boiling water and let soak, submerged, for 30 minutes. Drain, then seed, stem, and transfer to a blender. Add all remaining ingredients and blend at highest speed until completely smooth. Transfer to a small saucepan, bring to a simmer, and simmer for 5 minutes. Let cool, then refrigerate. Can be completed up to one week in advance of using. *Makes 1 cup.*

Pacific Flavors Salad

CHAPTER 2

Crunchy, Crispy Crackling Salads

One autumn day in the ancient northern Thai city of Chiang Mai, with the air clear and crisp, we spent several hours at an idyllic orchid farm surrounded by rice paddies. Around the corner of one of the old buildings, we discovered a typical Thai open-air kitchen and eating area. The smell of honey-coated chicken grilled over wood drifted to us, as several generations of women worked side by side preparing other regional specialties. Our thoughts turned immediately to lunch, in this spot of tranquillity where, stimulated by a succession of small salads, we recalled recent adventures riding elephants through tropical rain forests, taking early-morning pilgrimages to gold-encrusted temples, and treasure-shopping at the Night Bazaar.

Whether served in simple surroundings, like those we encountered in Chiang Mai, or amid the frenetic activity of food vendors in Singapore, or even high in the mountains of Bali, the salads of the South Seas blend greens enlivened with tangy, spicy dressings. Try these salads as appetizers, as first courses, or as palate cleansers following the entrée. Or make one of these salads a main course and accompany it with a New Wave Soup (see Chapter 3) and crusty bread, followed by a Sinful Sweet (Chapter 7).

Pacific Flavors Salad

4–6 cups baby salad greens
2 papayas, slightly underripe
1/3 cup pine nuts
2 ounces rice sticks
   (see glossary)
2 cups flavorless cooking oil
1 nutmeg

DRESSING
2 teaspoons finely minced or
   grated orange or tangerine
   zest
1/3 cup fresh orange or
   tangerine juice
1/3 cup balsamic vinegar
1/3 cup olive oil
   (not extra-virgin)
2 tablespoons light soy sauce
1/2 teaspoon Asian chile sauce
2 tablespoons finely minced
   ginger
3 tablespoons minced cilantro
   sprigs
3 tablespoons minced fresh
   mint leaves

Baby lettuce greens that just a few years ago were viewed as an exotic item found only in the most upscale California markets are now available nearly everywhere throughout the year. Perfectly clean and with a colorful mix of mild and the more bitter field greens, they make a great starting point for constructing salads. For this recipe, you might substitute another dressing, or toss in meat from a barbecued or roasted chicken to transform the dish into an entrée. Or deep-fry thin strips of wontons rather than using the crisp rice sticks. Serve this salad as a light appetizer to stimulate the palate, or after the entrée as a palate-cleansing prelude to a rich dessert; or have it as an after-theater nibble, washed down with Champagne to sustain an evening of romance.

ADVANCE PREPARATION

Keep salad greens refrigerated. Heat oven to 325°. Using a potato peeler, peel the papaya; cut in half and scoop out and discard the seeds. Cut flesh into 1/2-inch cubes and refrigerate. Spread pine nuts on a baking sheet and toast until they are light golden, about 8 minutes. Place the rice sticks in a large paper bag and separate into small bundles (the bag keeps things neat). Place the cooking oil in a 10-inch sauté pan over medium-high heat. Heat the oil until the end of a rice stick expands immediately when plunged into the oil. Add a small bundle of rice sticks. The moment they expand, about 3 seconds, turn the rice sticks over using tongs and cook on the other side another 3 seconds; remove and drain on paper towels. Repeat with remaining rice sticks. Store in a paper bag at room temperature. Set aside the nutmeg with a cheese grater or nutmeg grater. In a small bowl, combine all the dressing ingredients. Stir and refrigerate. *Can be completed to this point up to 8 hours in advance of serving.*

SERVING

Place the lettuce greens and papaya in a very large mixing bowl. Whisk the dressing and pour over salad; toss until evenly mixed. Gently fold in the crisp rice sticks, trying to keep them in as large pieces as possible. Transfer the salad to salad or dinner plates. Sprinkle on the nuts. Using a cheese grater, grate a little dusting of nutmeg over each salad. Serve at once.

Serves: 4 to 8 as a salad course.

Tex-Mex Salad with Ginger Dressing

3 ears sweet corn, husked
$^1/_3$ pound jicama
3 vine-ripened tomatoes
4 ounces soft goat cheese
2 corn tortillas
1 cup flavorless cooking oil
2 ripe avocados
4 cups bite-size pieces
  mixed salad greens

DRESSING
1 clove garlic, minced
2 tablespoons finely minced
  ginger
3 tablespoons chopped
  cilantro sprigs
$^1/_3$ cup extra-virgin olive oil
2 tablespoons balsamic vinegar
2 tablespoons light soy sauce
$^1/_2$ teaspoon Asian chile sauce
$^1/_2$ teaspoon grated or
  finely minced orange peel

During the summer, when corn is at its peak of tenderness, cut the kernels off the cob and toss them raw into your salad. With each bite, the sweet juice bursts from the crunchy kernels. You can quickly turn the salad into an entrée by adding cooked shrimp or barbecued chicken. Or drizzle the salad dressing across pieces of roast chicken that have been chilled and sliced.

ADVANCE PREPARATION

Stand the ears of corn on their ends and cut off the kernels. Peel the jicama and cut into thin, bite-size rectangles. Seed the tomatoes, then cut just the outside section into $^1/_2$-inch chunks. Crumble goat cheese and refrigerate until ready to use. Cut the tortillas into $^1/_4$-inch-wide slices. Place the oil in a 10-inch sauté pan, heat until a tortilla strip bounces across the surface when added, then fry the strips until light golden; immediately drain on paper towels. Set aside the avocado and greens. Combine the dressing ingredients, mix well, and refrigerate. *Can be completed to this point up to 8 hours in advance of Last-Minute Assembly.*

LAST-MINUTE ASSEMBLING

Seed, peel, and thinly slice the avocados. Place the corn, jicama, tomato, avocado, and greens in a bowl. Stir the dressing well; toss the salad with only enough dressing to lightly coat the greens. Gently stir in the tortilla strips and sprinkle on the goat cheese on top. Serve at once.

MENU IDEAS: A Saturday-night dinner for six—Barbecued Veal Chops with Macadamia Nuts (page 97) served with rice pilaf, Tex-Mex Salad, and for dessert, Chocolate Decadence (page 166).

Serves: 2 as an entrée, or 4 to 6 as a salad course.

Goat Cheese Salad with Ginger and Macadamia Nuts

5 ounces soft goat cheese, chilled

3 ounces roasted macadamia nuts

6 cups lettuce greens, preferably baby leaves

1 tablespoon extra-virgin olive oil

DRESSING

1 tablespoon finely minced ginger

½ clove garlic, finely minced

¼ cup chopped cilantro sprigs

7 tablespoons extra-virgin olive oil

3 tablespoons Japanese rice vinegar, unseasoned

¼ teaspoon salt

⅛ teaspoon freshly ground black pepper

When we are at home in Napa Valley, even the slightest mention of the famed Mustard's Restaurant is enough to provoke a short drive to sample their smoked barbecue ribs, grilled fish, and salads made from baby greens pulled from the rich Napa soil that day. This recipe is based on one of their most popular dishes. The soft goat cheese is cut into thin slices, rolled in chopped nuts, and panfried in a little olive oil before being placed on a bed of tiny lettuce greens. You can vary the choice of nuts, substituting raw crushed almonds or pecans, but be sure to purchase soft goat cheese, so the nuts will adhere to its surface.

ADVANCE PREPARATION

Carefully cut the goat cheese into four thin slices. If the nuts are salted, rinse briefly and pat dry. Place the nuts in a food processor and chop coarsely, then transfer to a plate. Coat each cheese slice with the nuts and refrigerate. If using large lettuce, tear into bite-size pieces. Refrigerate the lettuce. Set aside the olive oil. Combine the dressing ingredients and mix well. *Can be completed to this point up to 8 hours in advance of Last-Minute Assembling.*

LAST-MINUTE ASSEMBLING

To serve, stir the dressing; toss the greens with half the salad dressing. Arrange on four plates. Place a 12-inch skillet over medium-high heat. When hot, add the tablespoon of olive oil. Heat the oil, then gently add the goat-cheese slices. Sauté on both sides until the cheese is just heated through and the nuts are golden brown, about 2 minutes. Gently transfer to the center of the greens. Stir remaining dressing and spoon over the goat cheese and greens. Serve at once.

MENU IDEAS: For a Mustard's Restaurant-style lunch serving four—Goat Cheese Salad with Ginger and Macadamia Nuts, Smoked Baby Back Ribs with Pacific Flavors Barbecue Sauce (page 105) served with New Wave Garlic Bread (page 147), and ice cream with Raspberry Cabernet Sauvignon Sauce (page 160).

Serves: 4 as a salad course.

Asian Roasted Red Pepper Salad

Layers of roasted red pepper, feta cheese, and basil glisten in an extra-virgin olive oil dressing accented with fresh ginger. Vivid colors contrast with white plates; rich textural interplays create a succession of intriguing bites; and a simple combination of salad-dressing ingredients causes dramatic taste explosions. Asian Roasted Red Pepper Salad is a great beginning to a party, whether served as an appetizer or as a first course.

1 large red bell pepper
16 basil leaves
2 ounces Greek feta cheese
1 lime

DRESSING
1 clove garlic, very finely minced
1 tablespoon very finely
  minced ginger

¼ cup extra-virgin olive oil
2 tablespoons Japanese rice
  vinegar, unseasoned
1 teaspoon dark sesame oil
½ teaspoon freshly ground
  black pepper
¼ teaspoon salt

ADVANCE PREPARATION

Roast the pepper by placing it directly on a gas burner with the flame on the highest setting, or place the pepper under the broiler. Roast until blackened on all sides. Place the pepper in a plastic bag and let sit for 15 minutes. Peel off the blackened skin, seed, stem, and cut into 1-inch cubes. Set aside the basil. Slice the feta into 8 slices. Cut the lime into wedges. Combine the dressing ingredients. *Can be completed to this point up to 8 hours in advance of Last-Minute Assembly.*

LAST-MINUTE ASSEMBLY AND SERVING

Place a piece of pepper on a small salad plate. Add a slice of feta, 2 basil leaves, then another layer of pepper, feta, and basil. Repeat for remaining 3 servings (or divide the ingredients between 2 plates for an entrée). Refrigerate. Can be completed up to 2 hours before serving. To serve, shake the dressing. Drizzle the dressing over the salad. Serve with wedges of lime to squeeze over the salad.

Serves: 4 as a first course, or 2 as a light dinner salad.

Asian Roasted Red Pepper Salad

Asian Grilled Chicken Salad

4 chicken-breast halves,
  boned and skinned
6 cup baby lettuce greens
$\frac{1}{2}$ cup slivered almonds
2 ounces rice sticks
2 cups flavorless cooking oil

DRESSING
$\frac{1}{2}$ cup red-wine vinegar
$\frac{1}{4}$ cup light soy sauce
$\frac{1}{4}$ cup dark sesame oil
2 tablespoons plus 2
  teaspoons sugar
2 tablespoons hoisin sauce
2 teaspoons dry mustard
1 teaspoon Asian chile sauce
$\frac{1}{2}$ teaspoon salt
$\frac{1}{4}$ cup finely minced ginger
2 cloves garlic, finely minced

Salad dressings make great marinades for chicken, pork, veal, and all seafood destined for the barbecue. Because of the acidity, marinate for only 15 to 30 minutes or the dressing will begin to "cook" the meat or seafood. When serving this salad, if we are eating very informally, I'll grill the chicken at the last minute, then immediately cut it into strips and arrange these across the top of each person's salad. However, if this last-minute attention does not appeal to you, the salad is excellent when the chicken is grilled hours in advance and refrigerated.

ADVANCE PREPARATION

Place the chicken in a bowl. If the greens are in large pieces, tear into bite-size pieces; refrigerate. Heat the oven to 325°; spread almonds on a baking sheet and toast until golden, about 15 minutes. Combine dressing ingredients in a small bowl and whisk vigorously; divide in half. Refrigerate half the dressing. Pour the other half of the dressing over the chicken. Marinate for 15 minutes. Meanwhile, heat a grill pan over medium heat or prepare an outdoor barbecue to medium. Grill the chicken for 3 to 4 minutes on each side, until when you cut into a breast it has just lost its pink color in the center. Remove chicken from the grill, cool to room temperature, cut into $\frac{1}{4}$-inch-wide strips, and refrigerate.

    Place the rice sticks in a large paper bag and pull apart into small bundles. Heat the oil in a 10-inch skillet and cook the rice sticks as described on page 46. *Can be completed to this point up to 8 hours in advance of Last-Minute Assembling.*

LAST-MINUTE ASSEMBLING

Bring the chicken to room temperature. Place in a very large salad bowl with the greens and almonds. Shake reserved dressing and add half to the salad. Toss immediately. If the greens look dry and do not have enough flavor, add a little more dressing. Gently fold in the rice sticks, being careful not to crush them. Serve at once.

MENU IDEAS: Asian Grilled Chicken Salad, a wild-rice soup with corn-stick muffins, and a peach cobbler.

Serves: 4 as an entrée, or 6 to 8 as a salad course.

Melrose Mushroom Salad

1 pound mixed mushrooms
  (button, shiitake, portobello,
  enoki, oyster)
1/2 pound jicama
1 red bell pepper
3 cups bean sprouts
6 tablespoons chopped fresh
  parsley

DRESSING
2 tablespoons thinly sliced
  ginger
1 clove garlic
1/4 cup chopped green onions,
  white and green parts
5 tablespoons white-wine
  vinegar
1/4 cup olive oil (not
  extra-virgin)
2 tablespoon dark sesame oil
2 tablespoons oyster sauce
2 teaspoons sugar
1/4 teaspoon freshly ground
  black pepper

Wild mushrooms, once hidden deep under composts of oak leaves, thrusting up through soil in shady pine forests, or clinging to rotting stumps, are now conveniently packaged and sold in the produce section of most supermarkets. This beautiful photograph (overleaf) of shiitake, enoki, honey, button, cloud ear, and oyster mushrooms shows some of the choices to consider when making the salad. An easy-to-prepare dressing of sesame oil, oyster sauce, and garlic perfectly accents the varying textures of the mushrooms.

ADVANCE PREPARATION

Cut the button mushrooms into thin slices. Discard stems from the shiitake mushrooms and cut the caps into eighths. Cut the dirty ends off the enoki mushrooms and separate the long stems. Cut the oyster mushrooms into quarters or eighths. Place all the mushrooms in a bowl and refrigerate. Peel the jicama. Cut into bite-size rectangles about 1/4 inch thick. Cut the pepper into pieces the same size. Do not wash the bean sprouts. Chop the parsley. In separate containers refrigerate the jicama, pepper, sprouts, and parsley.

With the motor running, drop the ginger and garlic down the feed tube of a food processor fitted with the metal blade, and mince finely. Add the remaining dressing ingredients and blend for 30 seconds. *Can be completed to this point up to 8 hours in advance of Last-Minute Assembling.*

LAST-MINUTE ASSEMBLING

About 30 minutes before serving, toss the mushrooms in the dressing. Just before serving, stir in the jicama, pepper, sprouts, and parsley. Serve at once.

MENU IDEAS: A quick dinner for four—salmon fillet marinated in soy sauce, lemon, and ginger, then steamed or broiled and served with steamed rice; Melrose Mushroom Salad placed on a bed of lettuce greens; and fresh fruit.

Serves: 4 to 6 as a salad course.

OVERLEAF: Ingredients for Melrose Mushroom Salad

Peanut Ginger Noodle Salad

½ pound dried spaghetti-style
  noodles
1 bunch asparagus, tough ends
  removed
1 red bell pepper
10 red radishes
½ hothouse cucumber
2 cups bean sprouts

DRESSING
⅓ cup top-quality salted peanut
  butter
¼ cup fresh orange juice
¼ cup white-wine vinegar
2 tablespoons dark soy sauce
2 tablespoons dark sesame oil
1½ tablespoons sugar
1 teaspoon Asian chile sauce
¼ cup minced green onions,
  white and green parts
2 tablespoons finely minced
  ginger
1 clove garlic, finely minced

Salads make great appetizers. If friends are delayed or unforeseen events occur in the kitchen, you have a fairly substantial dish to accompany before-dinner drinks. Peanut Ginger Noodle Salad, with its assortment of crunchy vegetables and rich sweet-pungent peanut dressing, tickles the palate in anticipation of later culinary surprises. To vary the taste, use a different combination of vegetables, or grind roasted cashews in a food processor until they become a butter and substitute this for the peanut butter. The salad is also excellent as an accompaniment to barbecued meats.

ADVANCE PREPARATION

Bring 4 quarts of water to a rapid boil; add the noodles and a sprinkling of salt. Cook until tender, according to package directions. Tip into a colander, rinse under cold water, and drain thoroughly.

    Bring 2 quarts of water to a boil; add asparagus. The moment they turn a bright green, transfer them to a bowl of iced water and chill. When chilled, pat dry and cut on a diagonal into 1-inch lengths. Seed, stem, and matchstick-cut the pepper. Thinly slice the radishes. Seed and matchstick-cut the cucumber. Combine all the vegetables and refrigerate. In a bowl, combine the dressing ingredients and stir well; store at room temperature. *Can be completed up to this point 8 hours in advance of serving.*

SERVING

In a large bowl, combine the noodles and vegetables. Stir the dressing and pour over the noodles. Toss the noodles to evenly combine with the dressing. Transfer the salad to a platter or salad plates and serve at once.

Serves: 4 to 10 as an appetizer, or 6 as a salad course.

Thai Mango Salad

3 ripe mangos or slightly firm
  papayas
1 cup shredded hothouse
  cucumber
1 cup peeled and shredded
  jicama
1 small red bell pepper, seeded
  and shredded
1 cup raw cashews
1 cup flavorless cooking oil
1 head Bibb lettuce, torn into
  pieces

DRESSING
3 tablespoons minced fresh
  basil leaves
3 tablespoons minced fresh
  mint leaves
1 green onion, white and green
  parts, minced
2 tablespoons finely minced
  ginger
1 clove garlic, minced
3 tablespoons flavorless
  cooking oil
3 tablespoons fresh lime juice
2 tablespoons light brown sugar
2 tablespoons fresh orange juice
2 tablespoons Thai or
  Vietnamese fish sauce
2 teaspoons Asian chile sauce
1 teaspoon freshly grated
  nutmeg

We have often served this salad as an accompaniment to barbecued fish, chicken, and butterflied leg of lamb. The tropical flavors of mango, lime, and nutmeg provide a clean, sparkling taste, while the dramatic color contrasts and extraordinary crunch of the cashews are what make this salad so satisfying. Each guest cups a Bibb-lettuce leaf in his or her hand, adds a portion of the mango-salad mix, and then eats the salad-filled lettuce cup using the fingers.

ADVANCE PREPARATION

Using a small knife, peel the mangoes. Cut the flesh off in large pieces, then cut the pieces into ¼-inch-wide strips about 1 inch long; refrigerate. (If using papayas, peel with a potato peeler, scoop out the seeds, and cut the flesh into ½-inch cubes.) Prepare the cucumber, jicama, and pepper and refrigerate. Place the cashews and oil in a small saucepan. Set over medium-high heat and stir the cashews until they turn a light golden; immediately tip the cashews into a sieve placed over another saucepan. Pat the cashews dry and set aside; discard the oil. Separate the lettuce leaves; discard any large stems, and refrigerate. In a small bowl, combine the dressing ingredients; stir well and refrigerate. *Can be completed to this point up to 8 hours in advance of serving.*

SERVING

Place the mango, cucumber, jicama, pepper, and cashews in a large bowl. Stir the dressing, then pour it over the mango mixture. Gently stir, then transfer to a platter. Surround the platter with the lettuce leaves. Each person takes a lettuce leave, adds some of the mango salad, forms the lettuce leaf into a cup, and eats the salad filled lettuce cup using the fingers.

Serves: 4 to 6 as a salad course.

Tropical Paradise Salad

2 ripe avocados
Juice of 1 lemon or lime (optional)
2 vine-ripened tomatoes
2 ripe mangoes, peaches,
    nectarines, or papayas
4 cups baby lettuce greens
2 tablespoons unsalted roasted
    peanuts

DRESSING
3 tablespoons very finely
    minced ginger
¼ cup chopped basil leaves or
    cilantro sprigs
¼ cup fresh lime juice
3 tablespoons Thai or
    Vietnamese fish sauce
3 tablespoons light brown sugar
3 tablespoons flavorless
    cooking oil
½ teaspoon Asian chile sauce

Take this salad as a starting point and create your own tropical salad statement! Try adding one or more other fruits such as star fruit, kiwi, baby bananas, pears, and apples. We particularly like the latter two fruits, cut into wedges, brushed with an extra amount of the salad dressing, and cooked in a grill pan just before serving. Substitute roasted pine nuts for the peanuts, add one cup of cooked and chilled wild rice to the lettuce mix, or turn the salad into a main course by adding one pound of chilled cooked shrimp that has been shelled and deveined.

ADVANCE PREPARATION

Pit, peel, and thinly slice the avocados. If done ahead, squeeze a little lemon or lime juice over the avocado. Thinly slice the tomatoes. Peel the mangoes, then cut the flesh from the pits in large sections and slice thinly. Refrigerate the avocado, tomato, mango, and lettuce greens in separate containers. Place the peanuts in a food processor and chop finely. Combine the dressing ingredients, stirring well. *Can be complete to this point up to 8 hours in advance of Last-Minute Assembling.*

LAST-MINUTE ASSEMBLING

In a large bowl, combine the avocado, tomato, mango, and lettuce. Shake the dressing, pour over the salad, and toss all the salad ingredients until evenly coated. Transfer to a large platter or four to six salad plates. Sprinkle with peanuts and serve at once.

MENU IDEAS: A tropical dinner for six—chilled shrimp with Peanut Satay Sauce (page 41), Thai-High Barbecued Chicken (page 103) served with grilled potatoes, Tropical Paradise Salad, and Lemon Ice Cream (page 159).

Serves: 4 to 6 as the salad course.

Tropical Paradise Salad

Asian Shrimp Louis Salad

½ pound raw medium shrimp, peeled, deveined, and cut in half lengthwise
1 ripe avocado
Juice of ½ lemon (optional)
4 cups bite-size pieces mixed salad greens
1–2 cups assorted vegetables (optional), such as mushrooms, red pepper, zucchini, cucumber

DRESSING
½ cup mayonnaise
¼ cup heavy cream
3 tablespoons fresh lemon juice
1 tablespoon ketchup
1 tablespoon small (nonpareil) capers
1½ teaspoons Asian chile sauce
1 teaspoon Worcestershire sauce
1/4 cup chopped green onions, white and green parts
1 tablespoon finely minced ginger

At a restaurant near Kuta Beach, Bali, gray smoke from the open-air grilling swirls around members of a local dance troupe and obscures the image of the giant winged Garuda (a mythical bird) poised in the background, then finally drifts high into the wooden rafters. At the long buffet table, we helped ourselves to grilled fish wrapped in banana leaves, stir-fried rice flavored with tamarind and peanuts, and a "hill avocado salad," including shrimp and clumps of firm white fish tossed in a delicious Louis-type dressing. A line of ripe papaya slices ran down one side of the salad and a cooked lobster curled at the edge of the platter. This salad goes wonderfully with any barbecued meat or seafood and one of the side dishes from Chapter 6.

ADVANCE PREPARATION

Bring 2 quarts of water to a vigorous boil and add the shrimp. They are done when they turn white and curl, about 30 seconds. Check by cutting a shrimp in half; it should be white in the center. Immediately tip into a colander and then transfer to a bowl of ice water. Chill, pat dry, and set aside.

Seed, peel, and thinly slice the avocado. If done more than 30 minutes prior to serving, squeeze a little lemon juice over the avocado. Set the salad greens aside. If adding other vegetables, cut them into bite-size pieces. Combine the dressing ingredients and mix well. *Can be completed to this point up to 8 hours in advance of Last-Minute Assembling.*

LAST-MINUTE ASSEMBLING

Place the salad ingredients in a large bowl. Add the dressing and toss. Serve at once.

MENU IDEAS: A quick dinner for two—Asian Shrimp Louis Salad, New Wave Garlic Bread (page 147), and a summer melon served with lime wedges.

Serves: 2 as a main course, or 4 to 6 as a salad course.

Chicken Salad with Spicy Peanut Glaze

1 roast chicken, store-bought
4 cups bite-size pieces mixed
   salad greens
1 cup slivered hothouse
   cucumber (about 1
   cucumber)
1 cup slivered carrots
   (about 1 large carrot)
1 lime, cut into wedges
2 tablespoons mild olive oil,
   not extra-virgin

DRESSING
2 tablespoons minced shallots
4 cloves garlic, finely minced
1/2 cup peanut oil
3 tablespoons fresh lime juice
1/4 cup top-quality peanut butter
1/4 cup Thai or Vietnamese
   fish sauce
2 tablespoons honey
1 teaspoon Asian chile sauce

1/2 cup chopped mint or
   basil leaves, for garnish

Pyramids of tender chicken, jade cucumber, julienne carrots, and baby lettuce greens form a dramatic contrast. Guests spoon a little of the rich peanut dressing over the salad, sprinkle on chopped mint or basil, and finish with a squeeze of lime juice. This is a great way to begin a dinner, followed by Three Mushroom Soup served with hot dinner rolls, and concluding with ice cream topped with sliced strawberries. If you want to lessen last-minute preparation, make the salad dressing and the soup the day prior to the dinner.

ADVANCE PREPARATION

Discard the chicken skin and bones and pull the meat into bite-size pieces; refrigerate. Prepare the salad greens, cucumber, carrots, and lime wedges and refrigerate separately. Set aside the olive oil. Prepare the dressing: Place the shallots, garlic, and peanut oil in a small skillet over medium heat. Cook until the oil sizzles and the garlic turns white (do not let garlic brown; if it does, discard and begin again). Immediately tip out of pan and let cool. Transfer garlic and oil to a food processor along with the remaining dressing ingredients and blend thoroughly. Keep the dressing at room temperature. *Can be completed to this point up to 8 hours in advance of Last-Minute Assembling.*

LAST-MINUTE ASSEMBLING

Stir and taste the salad dressing. If it has become very thick, stir in a little cold water, and adjust the seasonings. To serve, toss the salad greens with the 2 tablespoons olive oil, then arrange the greens on four salad plates. Top with the vegetables and chicken. Serve the dressing in little bowls. Each person spoons the dressing over the salad ingredients, sprinkles on basil or mint, and squeezes lime juice over the salad.

Serves: 4 as a salad course, or 2 as an entrée.

Crazy Caesar Salad

Crazy Caesar Salad

2 heads romaine lettuce
8 tablespoons (1 stick) unsalted
  butter
4 cloves garlic, finely minced
1 teaspoon Asian chile sauce
1/2 teaspoon salt
2 cups stale bread, cut into
  1/2-inch cubes
1 red bell pepper
1/4 cup crushed unsalted
  roasted peanuts
1/2 cup grated imported
Parmesan cheese
1 lime

DRESSING
1/2 cup extra-virgin olive oil
1/4 cup fresh lemon juice
1 tablespoon oyster sauce
1 tablespoon mayonnaise
1/2 teaspoon each salt and
  freshly ground black pepper,
  or to taste

This is a crazy Caesar because we include grated lime zest, toasted peanuts, and chile-flavored croutons, and replace the anchovies with oyster sauce. Although many restaurants serve a chopped Caesar, for a bolder presentation use just the hearts of the romaine, keep the leaves whole, and after tossing the romaine with the dressing, position the leaves pointing in the same direction on large salad plates. The key to a great Caesar is the last-minute adjusting of the key flavor ingredients, namely extra-virgin olive oil, fresh lemon juice, salt, and freshly ground black pepper. Always taste, adjust the flavors, toss again, and repeat this process until the balance of flavors excites you.

ADVANCE PREPARATION

Pull off the large outer leaves of the romaine and set aside for another salad. Separate the tender interior leaves, then wash, dry, and refrigerate. Melt the butter in a 12-inch skillet over medium-high heat, add the garlic, and sauté for a few seconds until it sizzles. Stir in the chile sauce and add the bread cubes; sauté until well browned, about 8 minutes. Remove the croutons from the pan, sprinkle with salt, and set aside at room temperature.

Stem, core, and seed the pepper, then finely mince and refrigerate. Set aside the peanuts. Refrigerate the cheese. Set aside the lime. Place all the dressing ingredients in an electric blender and blend for a few seconds, until thoroughly mixed. Refrigerate the dressing. *Can be completed to this point up to 8 hours in advance of Last-Minute Assembling.*

LAST-MINUTE ASSEMBLING

Grate the cheese. Grate the lime skin, or remove the skin with a zester and finely mince. In a very large mixing bowl, position all the romaine leaves in the same direction. Shake the salad dressing. Pour the dressing over the leaves and gently toss the leaves until evenly coated with the dressing. Sprinkle the croutons, pepper, peanuts, lime zest, and half the cheese on top. Gently toss the lettuce leaves to evenly mix. Taste and adjust the seasonings, gently tossing the leaves again. Place the lettuce on four to six salad plates and sprinkle with the remaining Parmesan. Serve at once.

MENU IDEAS: Dinner for six to eight—Thai Fried Dumplings (page 36), Barbecued Veal Chops with Macadamia Nuts (page 97) served with roasted potatoes, Crazy Caesar Salad, and fresh berries with chocolate candies.

Serves: 4 to 6 as a salad course.

South Seas Beef Salad

½ pound beef fillet,
  trimmed of all fat
2 teaspoons dark soy sauce
2 teaspoons hoisin sauce
2 teaspoons dark sesame oil
5 cups bite-size pieces mixed
  salad greens
1 tablespoon flavorless
  cooking oil
1 nutmeg

DRESSING
1 clove garlic, finely minced
3 tablespoons chopped basil
  leaves or cilantro sprigs
½ teaspoon grated or finely
  minced orange zest
¼ cup fresh orange juice
3 tablespoons safflower oil
2 tablespoons fresh lime juice
1½ tablespoons light soy sauce
1 tablespoon honey
½ teaspoons Asian chile sauce

The flavors of this salad evoke memories of a dish served at the Water Garden Restaurant at the Royal Temple in Mengwi, Bali. We sat on a veranda overlooking the ancient canal and watched two old boatmen pulling a small passenger ferry across by ropes. The ethereal sounds of Balinese instrumental music filled the background as we gazed across the water at the lichen-covered stone walls surrounding the Hindu temple. Bites of sizzling beef placed on a bed of greens, and more orders of Bir Singh, intensified our anticipation of an afternoon visit to the monkey forest.

ADVANCE PREPARATION

Cut the meat against the grain into ⅛-inch-thin slices, then cut the slices in half. Combine the soy sauce, hoisin sauce, and sesame oil, add the meat, and marinate in the refrigerator for at least 15 minutes but not longer than 8 hours. Set aside the salad greens. Separately set aside the cooking oil and nutmeg. Combine all dressing ingredients, mix thoroughly, and refrigerate. *Can be completed to this point up to 8 hours in advance of Last-Minute Assembling.*

LAST-MINUTE ASSEMBLING

If the meat has been refrigerated, return to room temperature. Place the greens in a bowl, shake the dressing, then toss with the greens. Arrange on salad plates. Set a 12-inch skillet over high heat. When hot, add the cooking oil. When the oil just begins to smoke, add the beef and toss over high heat until the meat just loses its raw color on the outside, about 20 seconds. Immediately place the meat in the center of the salad greens on each plate. Grate a dusting of nutmeg over each salad. Serve at once.

MENU IDEAS: A casual dinner for four to eight—South Seas Beef Salad, Crazy Coconut Noodle Toss (page 132), and Chocolate Decadence (page 166). For this dinner, serve each dish as a separate course.

Serves: 2 as an entrée, or 4 to 6 as a salad course.

Asian Fruit Salad

½ cup shredded red bell pepper
2 slightly firm papayas or
    2 ripe mangos
2 ripe avocados
1 cup shredded hothouse
    cucumber (about ½ cucumber)
2 ripe bananas
4 cup baby lettuce greens or
    mild lettuce greens, torn
1 cup roasted macadamia nuts

DRESSING
3 tablespoons finely minced
    ginger
2 tablespoons minced fresh
    mint leaves
2 tablespoons minced cilantro
    sprigs
2 teaspoon finely minced or
    grated orange zest
1 teaspoon finely minced or
    grated lime zest
¼ cup fresh orange juice
2 tablespoons fresh lime juice
2 tablespoons Chinese rice wine
    or dry sherry
2 tablespoons honey
1 teaspoon Asian chile sauce

This refreshing salad is a good choice on a hot summer night, when served with an entrée such as Thai-High Barbecued Chicken or Asian Barbecued Salmon. Because of the soft texture of avocado, combine the cucumber, papaya, and red pepper first, toss with the salad dressing, and then gently add the avocado. The recipe gives directions for placing the fruit salad on lettuce greens that are lightly tossed with the dressing, but you can also serve the salad in bowls.

ADVANCE PREPARATION

Prepare the pepper. Using a potato peeler, peel the papayas, scoop out the seeds, and cut the flesh into ½-inch cubes. Cut each avocado in half and temporarily remove the pit. Using a small knife, cut down through the flesh to the skin, cutting the flesh into cubes; return the pit to the avocado, place the halves together, wrap with plastic wrap, and refrigerate. Prepare the cucumber. Refrigerate all ingredients, including the salad greens, in separate containers. If nuts are salted, rinse and pat dry, then coarsely chop. In a small bowl, combine all the dressing ingredients, stir well, and refrigerate. *Can be completed to this point up to 8 hours in advance of serving.*

SERVING

Peel and slice bananas. Place the greens in a large bowl. Stir the dressing, then add about 3 tablespoons of the dressing to the greens. Toss the greens, then transfer them to four salad plates. Unwrap the avocados, discard the pits, and with a spoon, scoop the avocado cubes into the bowl. Add all the remaining ingredients, including the dressing. Gently toss until evenly combined. Using a slotted spoon, place the fruit salad on the greens, and serve at once.

Serves: 4 as a dinner salad.

Thai Bouillabaise

CHAPTER 3

New Wave Soups

Few dishes evoke such strong positive childhood memories—of simple family dinners, and soothing tastes that mend the body. Yet all too often, soups go unconsidered when we plan to entertain or, if served, add to preparation and clean-up burdens in menus that are already overly complex. We hope this chapter restores soup to its rightful place at the table. Keep the menu simple, choose easy recipes, and do the preparation hours in advance. For example, any of these New Wave Soups is perfect as the main dish for a dinner. Begin with an easy appetizer, then, as an entrée, serve generous portions of soup accompanied by New Wave Garlic Bread (page 146) or California Cornbread (page 151); have a simple green salad, and conclude the meal with a Sinful Sweet (Chapter 7). Easy cooking, great food, and plenty of time for friends—this is the new wave of entertaining.

Choices in this chapter range from traditional Asian favorites, such as hot-and-sour soup and coconut-curry soup, to American and European standards with Asian twists. Goat cheese-filled wontons replace the traditional pork filling. Into the tomato broth of gazpacho goes papaya, ginger, lime, and Asian chile sauce; accents of dark sesame oil add a complex, nutty flavor to a wild-mushroom soup. Several of the soups are served chilled, and thus can be completed entirely ahead of time, while it takes only minutes to complete the final cooking steps of all the others. And you can increase every soup multiple times to serve larger groups.

Thai Bouillabaisse

Soup Broth
2 tablespoons olive oil
4 cloves garlic, minced
¼ cup minced shallots
1 tablespoon finely minced
    ginger
4 cups chicken broth, preferably
    homemade (page 69)
3 cups unsweetened coconut
    milk
½ cup dry white wine
2 tablespoons Thai or
    Vietnamese fish sauce
1 teaspoons Asian chile sauce
Large pinch of saffron

Final Soup Additions
20 small mussels
½ pound raw medium shrimp
½ pound skinless salmon fillet
½ pound vine-ripened tomatoes
2 tablespoons cornstarch
⅓ cup shredded fresh basil
    leaves
Salt to taste
Freshly grated nutmeg

Although this is one of the few time-consuming recipes in the book, nearly all the preparation can be completed hours in advance, and the last-minute assembling requires only about ten minutes of attention. Make the bouillabaisse the main course and surround it with other dishes that do not require any last-minute cooking. A good menu for six would be Goat Cheese with Pacific Flavors Rub, then the bouillabaisse accompanied by New Wave Garlic Bread, followed by a simple green salad tossed with an oil-and-vinegar dressing and dusted with imported Parmesan, and concluded with a dessert contributed by a dinner guest.

ADVANCE PREPARATION

Have ready all ingredients for the soup broth. Place a 4-quart saucepan over medium heat. Add the olive oil, garlic, shallots, and ginger. Sauté until the garlic sizzles and turns white, then add the remaining broth ingredients. Bring to a low boil, reduce the heat to low, and simmer for 30 minutes. Cool to room temperature and, if completed hours in advance, refrigerate the soup in its saucepan.

Scrub the mussels, pulling away the beards from between the shells. Shell, devein, and split the shrimp in half. Cut the salmon into bite-size pieces. Refrigerate the seafood in separate containers. Seed and chop the tomatoes. *Can be completed to this point up to 8 hours in advance of Last-Minute Cooking.*

LAST-MINUTE COOKING

Combine the cornstarch with an equal amount of cold water. Set aside the shredded basil. Bring the soup to a simmer. Transfer 2 cups of the soup liquid to a 3-quart saucepan and bring to a rapid boil. Add the mussels, cover, and cook until they open, about 5 minutes. Discard any mussels that do not open; then strain the liquid through a fine-meshed sieve back into the soup. Reserve the mussels.

Bring the soup to a low boil. Stir the cornstarch mixture into the soup. Add the shrimp, salmon, tomatoes, and basil. Simmer until salmon just begins to flake, about 1 minute. Taste and adjust the seasonings, particularly for chile sauce and salt. Add the mussels still in their shells. Pour into a soup tureen or individual bowls. Grate a little nutmeg over the top of the soup and serve at once.

Serves: 4 as an entrée, or 6 to 8 as a soup course.

Homemade Chicken Broth

3 pounds chicken wings
2 or 3 thin slices ginger
  (optional)
Garlic peels from a few cloves
1 green onion, white and green
  parts (optional)

Why broil trays of beef bones, search throughout the city for perfectly fresh veal knuckle bones, or lug home pounds of fish heads for stock? Most people will not be able to tell the slightest difference when a recipe calls for beef, veal, or fish stock and you substitute homemade chicken broth. Everyone will applaud just as vigorously. A couple of times a year, make a big batch of chicken broth. After it has simmered gently for a few hours, strain and refrigerate the broth. Once it has chilled, discard the hard layer of fat laying on the surface, then package the broth in small plastic bags and toss these into the freezer, where they stay will until needed. Start with chicken wings, perhaps augmented by other poultry and pork scraps, and simmer them in a big pot so that gradually the bone, marrow, and meat essences creep into the liquid: Now that's a broth to cure the common cold!

ADVANCE PREPARATION

Rinse the chicken wings in cold water and drain. Place in a large stockpot. Add enough cold water to cover by 2 inches. Place over high heat and bring to a very low boil. Reduce the heat to low and skim off any foam that rises to the surface. Add the ginger, if using, garlic skins, and green onion. Simmer the stock, partially covered, for 5 hours, periodically adding more water, if necessary, to keep up the level.

    Pour the broth through a colander lined with a kitchen towel or dampened cheesecloth and discard the solids. (The chicken meat will be of no use because all the flavor will have escaped into the broth.) Set the bowl aside and let the broth cool to room temperature before refrigerating.

    After refrigerating the broth overnight, scrape off and discard the hard layer of fat on the surface. Because the broth is highly perishable, place 1-cup amounts of the jellied broth in plastic food bags and freeze. The broth can be thawed and refrozen repeatedly.

Makes: 3 quarts (12 cups) rich chicken broth.

Asian Tropical Gazpacho

3 pounds vine-ripened tomatoes
1 cup chopped hothouse
   cucumber
1 ripe avocado
1/2 papaya, not overly ripe
1 green onion, white and green
   parts, minced
1/4 cup chopped fresh mint
   leaves or cilantro sprigs
3 tablespoons chopped fresh
   basil leaves
3 cloves garlic, very finely
   minced
3 tablespoons very finely minced
   ginger
3 tablespoons fresh lime juice
2 tablespoons Thai or
   Vietnamese fish sauce
2 teaspoons Asian chile sauce
1/2 teaspoon salt

TO SERVE
1/4 cup sour cream

The secret for this great-tasting soup is using vine-ripened tomatoes. Wait until they are available at the market or from your kitchen garden. The key technique is to seed the tomatoes over a sieve placed inside a bowl so that all the flavorful tomato juice can be captured and returned to the soup. Good recipe variations include substituting chunks of ripe mango for the papaya, or stirring chilled cooked shrimp or fresh lump crabmeat into the soup just prior to serving.

ADVANCE PREPARATION

Cut the tomatoes in half through their circumference (not down through the stem). Gently squeeze and shake each tomato half into a sieve placed in a bowl. Save all the juice. Cut away and discard the tomato stem area. Using a food processor, puree half the tomatoes and transfer to a bowl along with the reserved tomato juice. In the processor, coarsely chop the remaining tomatoes and transfer it to the bowl.

    Chop the cucumber in the processor and transfer it to the bowl. Pit the avocado, scoop out the flesh, and cut into bite-size pieces. Using a potato peeler, peel the papaya, then cut the papaya in half, discard the seeds, and cut the flesh into bite-size pieces. Add the avocado, papaya, green onion, mint, basil, garlic, ginger, lime juice, fish sauce, chile sauce, and salt to the bowl. Refrigerate. *Can be completed to this point up to 8 hours in advance of Last-Minute Serving.*

SERVING

To serve, taste the soup and adjust the flavors of chile, lime, and salt. Ladle the soup into bowls and top each bowl with a dollop of sour cream. Serve at once.

Serves: 2 as an entrée, or 4 as a soup course.

Scallop Thread Soup

1/3 pound fresh sea scallops
6 thin slices fresh ginger
6 cups chicken broth, preferably homemade (page 69)
2 green onions, white and green parts
1 red bell pepper
12 cilantro sprigs
2 large eggs
1 tablespoon Chinese rice wine or dry sherry
Juice from 1/2 lemon
2 tablespoons dark sesame oil
1/4 teaspoon freshly ground white pepper
1 teaspoon salt or to taste

Years ago a small band of us traveling through China found our way to a famous Suzhou establishment, the Moon in View Restaurant, where we enjoyed this soup. About to close for the evening, the management crowded us around a big circular table pushed up against tall windows facing a busy street. Our presence created a sensation. For two hours the gathering audience outside watched our chopsticks flash. Fresh quail on water spinach, crisp eel in caramelized sauce . . . the press of blue-clothed bodies close to our chairs . . . Suzhou carp rolls, stewed turtle . . . faces pressed flat against the restaurant windows . . . sweet-and-sour whole fish . . . tiny babies held high by mothers to view the "barbarians" . . . Scallop Blossom Soup, sweet-bean pastries, and giant peaches . . . waiters pushing through the crowd to deliver tall celadon-colored bottles of beer . . . later, a walk down darkened sycamore-lined lanes toward our beds ended another day of China surprises.

ADVANCE PREPARATION

Pull off and discard the little muscle that lies on one side of each scallop. Combine scallops, ginger, and broth in a large saucepan. Bring to a low simmer, cover, and cook for 1 hour. Discard the ginger and press the scallops with the back of the fork in the soup so they break apart into little threads. Set aside.

Shred the green onions. Stem, seed, and chop the red pepper. Set both aside with the cilantro. *Can be complete to this point up to 8 hours in advance of Last-Minute Assembling.*

LAST-MINUTE ASSEMBLING

Bring the broth to a low boil. Beat the eggs well, then stir 2 tablespoons of the hot soup into the eggs to warm them. Pour the eggs in a thin stream into the soup stock, stirring where they hit the hot liquid. Stir in the rice wine, lemon juice, sesame oil, and white pepper. Add salt to taste.

Pour the soup into a tureen or individual bowls. Stir in the green onions, red peppers, and cilantro. Serve at once.

MENU IDEAS: As a dinner for four, serve Scallop Thread Soup with California Cornbread (page 151), a large dinner salad, and a pineapple upside-down cake.

Serves: 2 as an entrée, or 4 to 6 as a soup course.

Wild Rice Seafood Soup

½ cup uncooked wild rice
1 pound raw large shrimp
1 large carrot
1 cup fresh or frozen sweet peas
½ block (7 ounces) bean curd
2 large eggs, well beaten

SOUP BROTH
6 cups chicken broth, preferably
   homemade (page 69)
3 tablespoons Chinese rice wine
   or dry sherry
2 tablespoons oyster sauce
1 tablespoon dark sesame oil
1 teaspoon Asian chile sauce
¼ cup minced green onion,
   white and green parts
3 tablespoons minced cilantro
   sprigs
2 tablespoons finely minced
   ginger
3 tablespoons cornstarch
Salt to taste

This easy soup makes a great main course, perhaps preceded by one of the dumplings from Chapter 1. Make the dumpling filling in the morning, involve your guests in the folding, then serve this soup accompanied by New Wave Garlic Bread. Encourage everyone to dunk the bread into the soup, which makes both the bread and soup taste even better! Follow this course with Crazy Caesar Salad, perhaps continuing the informal tone of the dinner by eating the baby romaine leaves using your fingers (the manner in which this salad was eaten originally). To conclude the dinner, serve the very easy Lemon Ice Cream, and decorate the dessert plates with a generous amount of Chocolate Grand Marnier Sauce and fresh berries.

ADVANCE PREPARATION

In a 2-quart saucepan, bring 5 cups of water to a low boil. Stir in the wild rice, add a dash of salt, turn heat to low, and simmer, covered, until the grains are tender, about 40 minutes. Immediately drain the rice into a sieve, rinse with cold water, and drain again. Transfer the rice to a bowl and refrigerate. Shell, devein, and split the shrimp in half; refrigerate. Peel the carrot and cut on a sharp diagonal into very thin slices; overlap the slices and cut into matchstick pieces; refrigerate. Set aside the peas in the refrigerator. Cut the bean curd into ½-inch cubes or thin rectangles, and refrigerate. Beat the eggs and refrigerate. In a 3-quart saucepan, combine the broth ingredients except the salt and cornstarch and refrigerate. *Can be completed to this point up to 8 hours in advance of Last-Minute Assembling.*

LAST-MINUTE ASSEMBLING

Combine the cornstarch with an equal amount of cold water. Bring the broth to a low boil. Stir in the wild rice, shrimp, carrot, peas, and bean curd. Bring to a low boil. Stir in the cornstarch mixture. Stir the eggs into the soup. Taste the soup and adjust the flavors, especially for salt. Turn the soup into a tureen or individual bowls. Serve at once.

Serves: 2 as an entrée, or 4 to 6 as a soup course.

Hot and Sour Sichuan Tomato Soup and New Wave Garlic Bread (recipe on page 147)

Hot and Sour Sichuan Tomato Soup

1 large vine-ripened tomato
1/2 block (7 ounces) bean curd
8 small button mushrooms
1 skinless, boneless chicken
   breast (6–8 ounces)
1 cup slivered carrots (about 1
   large carrot)
1/2 cup slivered green onions,
   white and green parts
   (about 2)
6 cups chicken broth, preferably
   homemade (page 69)
2 tablespoons cornstarch
2 large eggs

SEASONING MIX
6 tablespoons red wine vinegar
1 tablespoon dark soy sauce
1 tablespoon dark sesame oil
1 teaspoon finely ground white
   pepper
1 teaspoon salt
1/2 teaspoon Asian chile sauce

Hot-and-sour soup, with its thick blend of tofu, strips of tender meat, and ribbons of egg flowers, all accented with peppers and vinegar, is one of the world's great soups. Except for heating the soup, which takes only minutes, all the preparation can be completed hours in advance. Because everyone's tastes differ, go lightly on the seasonings, and instead accompany the soup with a white-pepper grinder or a little bowl of Asian chile sauce, as well as a pitcher of rice vinegar, so each person can adjust the spicy and sour tastes. As foreheads redden and perspire, serve a mild dish such as a cucumber-and-feta-cheese salad that has been lightly dressed with extra-virgin olive oil, and to drink, lots of Tsing Tao beer.

ADVANCE PREPARATION

Cut the tomato in half and squeeze out the seeds. Sliver the flesh. Cut the bean curd into bite-size pieces. Very thinly slice the mushrooms. Cut the chicken breast into very thin bite-size pieces. Set aside the carrots and the green onions. Separately set aside the broth, cornstarch, and eggs. In a small bowl, combine the seasoning mix. *Can be completed to this point up to 8 hours in advance of Last-Minute Cooking.*

LAST-MINUTE COOKING

Combine the cornstarch with an equal amount of cold water. Bring the broth to a low boil. Add the chicken, and give the soup a vigorous stir to separate the meat. Add the vegetables, bean curd, and seasoning mix. Bring the soup back to a low boil and stir in the cornstarch mixture. Beat the eggs well and add 2 tablespoons of hot soup to the eggs to warm them, then slowly pour the eggs into the soup while beating with a fork as they hit the hot broth. Remove from heat and adjust for salt, spice, and tartness. Turn into a soup tureen or individual bowls and serve.

MENU IDEAS: An easy dinner for four—Hot and Sour Sichuan Tomato Soup served with cornbread muffins, a spinach-walnut salad, and a fruit tart for dessert.

Serves: 4 as an entrée, or 6 to 8 as a soup course.

Chilled Yellow Tomato Soup with Ginger

12 vine-ripened yellow tomatoes
3 yellow bell peppers
1 yellow onion
1 bunch cilantro
5 cloves garlic, finely minced
2 tablespoons finely minced
  ginger
1 jalapeño
½ cup extra-virgin olive oil
½ cup white-wine vinegar
Salt to taste

Every summer, during the height of the tomato season, Teri makes this soup from perfectly ripe yellow tomatoes growing just outside our kitchen door—it takes only about thirty minutes to assemble and puree all the ingredients, and the soup has a striking yellow color speckled with flecks of cilantro. It is also very good made with red tomatoes, or transformed into a seafood soup by the last-minute addition of chilled cooked shrimp or fresh lump crabmeat.

ADVANCE PREPARATION

Cut tomatoes in half through the circumference, not through the stem. Gently shake out the seeds. Cut away the stem area, and cut the tomatoes into large cubes. Stem, seed, and cube the peppers. Peel and thickly slice the onion. Cut off and discard the large cilantro stems. Set aside a few sprigs of cilantro for a garnish. Set aside the garlic and ginger. Stem and very finely mince the jalapeño. Combine all the ingredients except the salt in a large bowl, then place about one-quarter of the mixture at a time in a food processor. Puree until completely liquefied, then transfer to a clean bowl. Taste and adjust the flavors, especially for salt and vinegar; then refrigerate. *Can be completed to this point up to 24 hours in advance of serving.*

SERVING

Taste the soup again and adjust for salt, spice, and vinegar. If you want a spicier soup, stir in a little Asian chile sauce. Serve in chilled bowls. Garnish with the cilantro sprigs.

Serves: 6 to 8 as a first course.

Goat Cheese Wonton Soup

1/4 cup cornstarch, for dusting

DUMPLINGS
1 tablespoon finely minced
 ginger
2 green onions, white and
 green parts, minced
1/2 pound raw shrimp, shelled
 and deveined
2 ounces soft goat cheese
1 tablespoon oyster sauce
30 wonton skins or round gyoza
 skins

SOUP MIX
10 fresh button mushrooms,
 caps tightly closed
10 spears asparagus
1/2 cup shredded carrot
 (1 medium carrot)
Shredded green onions or sprigs
 of cilantro, as garnish
6 cups chicken broth, preferably
 homemade (page 69)
1 tablespoon light soy sauce
1 tablespoon dark sesame oil
2 tablespoons cornstarch

Salt and freshly ground white
 pepper to taste

The flavor of this soup can be quickly modified by replacing 2 cups of the broth with coconut milk, a squeeze of lime juice, a stalk of lemongrass cut into one-inch lengths, and chile sauce or minced fresh red chiles. Whether you make this modification or not, these goat-cheese-filled wontons have a wonderful creamy texture and richness that is perfectly balanced by the broth. For more variations, try substituting raw salmon for the shrimp, or use one of the other dumpling fillings from Chapter 1.

ADVANCE PREPARATION

Line a baking sheet with parchment paper and dust with the cornstarch. Set aside. Prepare the dumplings: Combine the ginger and green onions in a mixing bowl. Place the shrimp in a food processor and mince. Add to the bowl along with the goat cheese and oyster sauce. Mix thoroughly. Fill the wonton skins and fold the dumplings as described on page 27. Place on the baking sheet and refrigerate.

Prepare the soup mix. Thinly slice the mushrooms. Snap off and discard the tough asparagus ends, then cut the asparagus on a sharp diagonal into 1-inch lengths. Prepare the carrots. Place the mushrooms, asparagus, and carrots in a container and refrigerate. Prepare the green onions or cilantro, and refrigerate. In a bowl, combine the broth, soy sauce, and sesame oil; refrigerate. Set aside the 2 tablespoons cornstarch. *Can be completed to this point up to 8 hours in advance of Last-Minute Assembling.*

LAST-MINUTE ASSEMBLING

Combine the 2 tablespoons cornstarch with an equal amount of cold water. Bring the broth to a simmer. Bring 6 quarts of water to a rolling boil and add the wontons; stir gently. As soon as the wontons float to the surface, in about 2 minutes, transfer to the broth. Bring the broth to a low boil and add the mushrooms, asparagus, and carrots. Cook until the asparagus brightens. With the soup at a low boil, stir in the cornstarch mixture.

Remove the soup from the stove. Add the salt and pepper to taste. Pour into a soup tureen or individual bowls, and garnish with the green onions or cilantro. Serve at once.

MENU IDEAS: As an entrée for four, serve this soup with garlic bread, a spinach-walnut salad, and for dessert, slices of chocolate cake with fresh strawberries.

Serves: 4 as an entrée, or 6 to 8 as a soup course.

Coconut Curry Soup Explosion

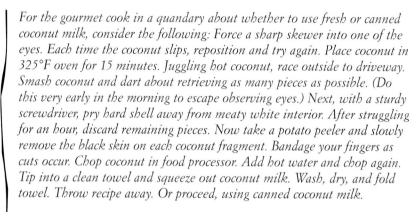

¼ pound soba noodles or dried thin spaghetti
2 teaspoons flavorless cooking oil
3 cups unsweetened coconut milk
2 cups chicken broth, preferably homemade (page 69)
2 tablespoons very finely minced ginger
3 tablespoons Thai or Vietnamese fish sauce
1 tablespoon curry powder
2 teaspoons grated or finely minced lime zest
2 tablespoons fresh lime juice
4 hot red chiles, seeded and slivered, or 2 teaspoons Asian chile sauce
4 skinless, boneless chicken breast halves
1 tablespoons dark sesame oil
8 button mushrooms, caps tightly closed
Salt to taste
Sprigs of cilantro, for garnish

For the gourmet cook in a quandary about whether to use fresh or canned coconut milk, consider the following: Force a sharp skewer into one of the eyes. Each time the coconut slips, reposition and try again. Place coconut in 325°F oven for 15 minutes. Juggling hot coconut, race outside to driveway. Smash coconut and dart about retrieving as many pieces as possible. (Do this very early in the morning to escape observing eyes.) Next, with a sturdy screwdriver, pry hard shell away from meaty white interior. After struggling for an hour, discard remaining pieces. Now take a potato peeler and slowly remove the black skin on each coconut fragment. Bandage your fingers as cuts occur. Chop coconut in food processor. Add hot water and chop again. Tip into a clean towel and squeeze out coconut milk. Wash, dry, and fold towel. Throw recipe away. Or proceed, using canned coconut milk.

ADVANCE PREPARATION

Bring 5 quarts of water to a rapid boil. Add the noodles and cook until tender in the center, about 5 minutes. Immediately drain, rinse with cold water, and drain again. Mix in the cooking oil and set aside. In a 3-quart saucepan, combine the coconut milk, broth, ginger, fish sauce, curry powder, lime zest and juice, and chiles or chile sauce. Refrigerate if completed more than 1 hour in advance of last-minute cooking. Cut the chicken into very thin bite-size pieces, toss with sesame oil, and refrigerate. Thinly slice the mushrooms and refrigerate. *Can be completed to this point up to 8 hours in advance of Last-Minute Cooking.*

LAST-MINUTE COOKING

Bring the soup to a simmer and cook over low heat for 20 minutes. Add the chicken and stir gently with a spoon to separate the pieces. Then add the mushrooms, noodles, and salt. Taste and adjust the seasonings, especially for salt. Turn into a soup tureen or individual bowls and garnish with cilantro sprigs. Serve at once.

MENU IDEAS: Serve this as an entrée accompanied by a simple salad. For a fun variation on this recipe, pass small bowls of freshly grated coconut, minced green onion, minced cilantro, wedges of lime, and chile sauce so guests can create their own flavor combinations.

Serves: 4 as an entrée, or 6 to 8 as a soup course.

Coconut Curry Soup Explosion

Chilled Avocado Soup with Ancho Chile Jam

2 ripe avocados
1/4 cup cilantro sprigs
1 clove garlic, minced
2 tablespoons finely minced ginger
2 tablespoons fresh lemon juice
1/2 teaspoon Asian chile sauce
1 teaspoon salt
1 1/2 cups canned low-sodium chicken broth
1/2 cup heavy cream
3 Bibb lettuce leaves

ANCHO CHILE JAM
1 ounce dried ancho chiles (about 3)
1 tablespoon red-currant jelly
2 teaspoons honey
1 teaspoon red or white vinegar
1/4 teaspoon salt
1 clove garlic, peeled
1 tablespoon minced shallot

One of my most vivid food memories is tasting chilled avocado soup while staying in the Mexican resort community of Cuernavaca as a high school student. The thick, rich, slightly spicy, emerald soup placed in rustic bowls and served in a tropical-garden setting complete with giant parrots observing our activities and tame monkeys stretching at their tethers created a kaleidoscope of exotic sensations. The soup is also very good with a half pound cooked and chilled shrimp or fresh lump crabmeat stirred in just before serving. For this soup, it's important to use canned chicken broth, as the homemade version will cause the soup to gel when chilled. Use a low-sodium broth so you can control the amount of salt.

ADVANCE PREPARATION

Cut the avocados in half, discard the seeds, and scoop out the flesh. Transfer to a food processor fitted with the metal blade and puree. Add cilantro, garlic, ginger, lemon juice, chile sauce, and salt. Process until liquefied. With the machine running, pour the cream and chicken broth down the feed tube. Transfer to a bowl, press plastic wrap across the surface of the soup, and refrigerate until thoroughly chilled. Tear lettuce into 2-inch pieces.

To make the jam, place the chiles in a bowl and cover with boiling water; soak until completely softened, about 30 minutes. Drain chiles, then stem, seed, and place them in a food processor fitted with the metal blade. Add remaining ingredients and process until a paste is formed. Transfer to a container, cover, and refrigerate. *Can be completed to this point up to 8 hours in advance of serving.*

SERVING

Transfer the soup to chilled soup bowls. Place 2 teaspoons of the jam in the center of each lettuce piece, and place these in the center of each bowl. Pass the additional jam and let each person swirl some into the soup. Serve at once.

Serves: 4 to 8 as a soup course.

Three Mushroom Soup

1 pound small fresh button
  mushrooms, caps closed
$\frac{1}{2}$ pound fresh shiitake
  mushrooms
$\frac{1}{4}$ pound fresh chanterelle or
  portobello mushrooms
1 bunch chives
2 cloves garlic, minced
1 tablespoon finely minced
  ginger
$\frac{1}{4}$ cup minced shallots
4 tablespoons ($\frac{1}{2}$ stick)
  unsalted butter
6 cups chicken broth, preferably
  homemade (page 69)
$\frac{1}{4}$ cup Chinese rice wine or dry
  sherry
1 tablespoon dark sesame oil
$\frac{1}{4}$ teaspoon white pepper
2 tablespoons cornstarch
Salt to taste

This rich-tasting mushroom soup is excellent as a main dish, accompanied by a green salad and a hearty dark bread. Variations we have enjoyed include substituting different types of mushrooms, such as fresh enoki, morels, and porcini mushrooms, adding thinly sliced leftover cooked meat just to reheat, or transforming the soup into a more substantial dish by stirring in three cups of cooked pasta. However you make this recipe, sauté the mushrooms with the total amount of butter called for, since this contributes a wonderful richness to the soup without any hint of oiliness. Also, sauté the mushrooms until all the moisture evaporates; this heightens the mushrooms' texture and intensifies their flavor.

PREPARATION AND COOKING

Wipe the mushrooms with a damp cloth. Cut the button mushrooms into $\frac{1}{8}$-inch slices. Discard the shiitake stems, and cut the caps into $\frac{1}{4}$-inch-wide strips. Cut the chanterelle mushrooms into $\frac{1}{8}$-inch thick slices. Cut the chives into 1-inch lengths and refrigerate. Combine the garlic, ginger, and shallots.

    Place a wide-bottomed saucepan over medium-high heat. Add the butter, garlic, ginger, and shallots. Sauté until the butter melts and the garlic sizzles, and then add the mushrooms. Sauté over low heat until they soften and all the moisture evaporates, about 10 minutes. Add the broth, rice wine, sesame oil, and white pepper. Bring to a low simmer, then cool to room temperature and refrigerate. *Can be completed to this point up to 8 hours in advance of Last-Minute assembling.*

LAST-MINUTE ASSEMBLING

Combine the cornstarch with an equal amount of cold water. Bring the soup to a low boil. Stir the cornstarch mixture into the soup. Taste and adjust seasonings (I usually add about $1\frac{1}{2}$ teaspoons salt). Stir in the chives and serve at once.

MENU IDEAS: This soup make a great entrée, but it is also excellent as a first course preceding one of the grilled-fish recipes from the next chapter.

Serves: 2 as an entrée, or 6 as a soup course.

Steamed Lobster with Herb Butters

CHAPTER 4

Seafood and Meats: Sizzling and Smoking

Cooking is a joyful, edible art, imbued with the spirit of creating and the gift of sharing. The beautiful foods used in this chapter, such as lobster, veal, lamb, and salmon, are matched with Asian seasonings to achieve fresh, innovative flavors and colors. Combinations of tropical ingredients give a special taste to grilled swordfish, add an exciting contrast to crisp southern fried chicken, form a caramel glaze around smoked rib-eye steaks, and become a crusty surprise on butterflied leg of lamb.

Nowhere in this book are such diverse Asian ingredients matched so often with food thought of as traditionally American as in this chapter. Using these recipes as a guideline, try inventing your own cross-cultural accents to everyday food: add fresh basil and hot chiles to a bubbling pot roast; broil sole rubbed with a dash of oyster sauce, sesame oil, and grindings of Sichuan pepper; sauté shiitake mushroom caps in butter, then place them on charbroiled hamburgers sandwiched between sesame-seed buns.

Steamed Lobster with Herb Butters

2 live lobsters, 1½ pounds each
Salt and freshly ground pepper
Lemon wedges

LEMON-GINGER BUTTER
8 tablespoons (1 stick) unsalted
  butter, at room temperature
2 tablespoons finely minced
  ginger
2 tablespoons finely minced
  fresh chives
4 teaspoons grated or finely
  minced lemon zest
½ teaspoon freshly ground
  black pepper
½ teaspoon Asian chile sauce
¼ teaspoon salt

CILANTRO-BASIL BUTTER
8 tablespoons (1 stick) unsalted
  butter, at room temperature
3 cloves garlic, finely minced
¼ cup finely minced cilantro
  sprigs
¼ cup finely minced basil leaves
½ teaspoon freshly ground
  black pepper

At least once a year we suffer a lobster "attack" that quickly results in the two of us cooking, cracking, and eating as many of these noble creatures from the depths as possible! The best-tasting lobster depends on three factors. First, buy ones that have just been pulled from the ocean or that have been kept in lobster tanks for only a short time. Second, cook the lobsters in only a few inches of rapidly boiling water so that they steam rather than submerging them in a pot full of boiling water. The latter technique results in watery, flavorless lobster meat. Third, a lobster overcooked by even 30 seconds becomes inedibly tough. Within a minute of the time lobster has turned bright red, it's perfectly cooked.

ADVANCE PREPARATION

Keep lobster refrigerated. Have ready salt, pepper, and lemon wedges. Place the ingredients for each flavored butter in a food processor and process until thoroughly blended. Transfer each to a small container and refrigerate. Or form the butter into a ½-inch-thick block. Refrigerate, then cut the butter into whimsical shapes. *Can be completed to this point up to 8 hours in advance of Last-Minute Cooking.*

LAST-MINUTE COOKING

Bring the herb butters to room temperature. In a 12-quart saucepan, bring 2 inches of water to a rapid boil over highest heat. Add the lobsters, head first, and cover the pot tightly. Cook for 8 minutes, then remove lobsters and cool for 5 minutes. Using a sturdy knife or poultry shears, cut the lobsters in half lengthwise. Or, twist off the tail and, using the tongs of a fork, pull out the tail meat. Crack the claws. Place each lobster on a heated dinner platter or plates. Accompany with the flavored butters and the lemon wedges. Eat at once.

MENU IDEAS: Dinner for four friends newly reunited—Asian Roasted Red Pepper Salad (page 50; double the recipe), Steamed Lobster with Herb Butters (double the recipe) served with hot rolls or garlic bread, and for dessert, Warm Chocolate Crème Brûlée (page 162).

Serves: 2 as an entrée.

Barbecued Salmon Steaks with Spicy Herb Coconut Sauce

4 fresh salmon steaks, 1–2 pounds
2 tablespoons light soy sauce
2 tablespoons Chinese rice wine or dry sherry
2 teaspoons dark sesame oil
1 lime

SAUCE
2 tablespoons flavorless cooking oil
2 tablespoons finely minced ginger
3 cloves garlic, finely minced
1 cup unsweetened coconut milk
2 tablespoons Thai or Vietnamese fish sauce
2 tablespoons Chinese rice wine or dry sherry
2 teaspoons cornstarch
$1/2$ teaspoon Asian chile sauce
$1/4$ cup chopped fresh basil leaves
$1/4$ cup chopped fresh mint leaves

Barbecued salmon looks spectacular placed in the center of this coconut-herb-infused sauce. For alternatives, substitute fresh tuna that is seared on a very hot barbecue and served still rare in the center. Or marinate chicken pieces for 30 minutes with soy sauce, sesame oil, and rice wine, then barbecue and serve with the sauce. Or sauté $1^{1}/_{2}$ pounds large shrimp, shelled and deeply butterflied, in the oil-ginger-garlic mixture from this recipe, and when they turn white, add the sauce. Bring to a boil, and cook the shrimp just until they lose any raw color in their centers. Served with roasted fingerling potatoes, and a simple salad of lettuce greens, this would be a terrific and easy-to-make weekend dinner.

ADVANCE PREPARATION

Refrigerate the salmon. In a small bowl, combine the soy sauce, rice wine, and sesame oil. Cut the lime into wedges and refrigerate. In a small bowl, combine the cooking oil, ginger, and garlic. In another small bowl, combine the remaining sauce ingredients, mix well, and refrigerate. *Can be completed to this point up to 8 hours in advance of Last-Minute Cooking.*

LAST-MINUTE COOKING

If using a gas barbecue, heat to medium (350°F). If using charcoal or wood, prepare the fire. When the coals or wood are ash-covered, rub the salmon on both sides with the soy-sauce mixture. Brush the grill with oil, then lay the salmon on the grill. Cook the salmon for about 3 minutes on each side. The salmon is done when it just begins to flake. Alternatively, broil the salmon about 3 minutes on each side. Keep the salmon warm while making the sauce.

Stir the sauce. Place a 10-inch sauté pan over medium-high heat. Add the oil-ginger mixture. When the ginger begins to sizzle but has not browned, add the sauce. Bring to a low boil. Taste and adjust the seasonings. Spoon the sauce onto four heated dinner plates. Position the salmon in the center of the sauce, and serve at once accompanied by lime wedges.

Serves: 4 as an entrée.

Thai Sauteed Shrimp

1 pound raw large shrimp
2 tablespoons flavorless
  cooking oil
4 cloves garlic, minced
3 small fresh hot chiles, minced
¼ cup fresh basil leaves
¼ cup fresh mint leaves
2 teaspoons grated or minced
  lime zest
Juice from 1 lime
1 tablespoon Thai or
  Vietnamese fish sauce
2 teaspoons light brown sugar
½ teaspoon cornstarch

Welcome to Bangkok—city of klongs *and* wats, *modern office buildings and ancient ruins, saffron-robed monks and busy executives, gleaming spires of royal buildings and tin shacks lining water hyacinth–choked waterways, and terminal traffic gridlock—the pleasure capital of the world. Our three-wheeled* tuk tuk, *decorated with orchid garlands and ornate tin molding, slipped between dented taxis, raced past diesel-belching trucks, and dared pedestrians to cross Silom Road. Moments later, shielded from the city chaos by a high garden wall at Thanying Restaurant, we feasted on a spicy seafood soup, chicken curry with green eggplant, tiny spring rolls wrapped with lettuce, and freshwater prawns sautéed with herbs, chiles, and fish sauce. For a dinner for two, Crazy Coconut Noodle Toss is a good accompaniment to this shrimp dish.*

ADVANCE PREPARATION

Shell the shrimp, cut deeply along the top, and rinse out the vein; refrigerate. Combine the cooking oil with the garlic and minced chiles. Refrigerate the basil with the mint. In a small bowl, combine the lime zest, lime juice, fish sauce, brown sugar, and cornstarch; refrigerate. *Can be completed to this point up to 8 hours in advance of Last-Minute Cooking.*

LAST-MINUTE COOKING

Mince the basil and mint. Place a 12-inch skillet over highest heat. When very hot, add the cooking oil with garlic and chiles, then sauté for 15 seconds. Add the shrimp and sauté over highest heat until they turn white, about 2 minutes. Add the herbs and cook for 15 seconds more. Stir in the lime juice mixture. Taste and adjust the seasonings. Serve at once.

Serves: 2 as an entrée.

Thai Sautéed Shrimp

Grilled Swordfish with Ginger-Cilantro Butter Sauce

2 pounds fresh swordfish
Marinade from Asian Barbecued
  Salmon (page 92)

SAUCE
²/₃ cup dry white wine
¹/₄ cup white wine vinegar
1 tablespoon finely minced
  ginger
1 small shallot, minced
¹/₂ pound (2 sticks) unsalted
  butter, at room temperature
1 teaspoon grated or minced
  lemon zest
¹/₄ cup finely minced cilantro
  sprigs
¹/₄ teaspoon freshly ground
  white pepper, or more
  to taste
¹/₄ teaspoon salt

Swordfish is so lean its interior quickly turns from perfectly moist to dry and unpalatable. To prevent this, always buy it very fresh. Ask the fishmonger to cut the steaks into individual 6- to 8-ounce pieces at least 1 inch thick (thinner pieces never taste moist). There is an easy trick to telling when swordfish is perfectly cooked. Lift the swordfish off the grill with a spatula and with the other hand press down on the edge of the swordfish. The moment it's perfectly cooked, little fracture lines will appear across the top.

ADVANCE PREPARATION

Keep swordfish refrigerated. Combine and refrigerate the marinade. Place the wine, vinegar, ginger, and shallot in a small nonreactive saucepan. Bring to a rapid boil over high heat and reduce until just 4 tablespoons remain. Set aside and refrigerate. *Can be completed to this point up to 8 hours in advance of Last-Minute Cooking.*

LAST-MINUTE COOKING

Place the swordfish in a nonreactive container. Stir the marinade and pour it over the swordfish, turning the pieces to coat evenly. Marinate for 30 minutes, refrigerated. If using a gas barbecue, heat to medium (350°F). If using charcoal or wood, prepare the fire. When the coals or wood are ash-covered, place the fish in a grilling basket. Grill the fish over medium-high heat until it just begins to flake, about 8 minutes. Turn once during barbecuing and brush with the remaining marinade. Transfer the fish to heated dinner plates or a serving platter.

    Cut the butter into 16 pieces. Bring the wine-vinegar mixture to a rapid boil over medium-high heat, then add the butter all at once and beat vigorously with a whisk. When just a few lumps of butter remain (about 20 seconds after adding), pour the sauce into a bowl. Stir in the lemon zest, cilantro, pepper, and salt. Taste and adjust the seasoning, adding more pepper if necessary. Spoon the sauce around the fish and serve at once.

MENU IDEAS: For a dinner serving four, accompany with a rice pilaf, a tomato-and-avocado salad, and a hot peach crisp for dessert.

Serves: 4 as an entrée.

Grilled Swordfish with Ginger-Cilantro Butter Sauce

Ingredients for Sautéed Crab with Basil Lemongrass Sauce

Sauteed Crab with Basil Lemongrass Sauce

4 soft-shell crabs, cleaned by the fishmonger, or ³/₄ pound fresh lump crabmeat
¹/₄ pound button mushrooms
1 red bell pepper or small fresh red chile
1 cup slivered basil leaves
2 cups bean sprouts
2 tablespoons finely minced ginger
2 cloves garlic, minced
1 tablespoon minced lemongrass stem (optional)
2 tablespoons unsalted butter
2 tablespoons flavorless cooking oil

SAUCE
¹/₄ cup chicken broth, preferably homemade (page 69)
¹/₄ cup Chinese rice wine or dry sherry
2 tablespoons oyster sauce
2 teaspoons grated or finely minced lemon zest
2 teaspoons cornstarch
¹/₄ teaspoon sugar
¹/₄ teaspoon freshly ground black pepper
¹/₄ cup chopped fresh basil leaves

When Teri and I have led groups to the Far East on eating adventures, I have seen Americans dumbfounded when a platter of sautéed crabs, with the body and legs cracked and the shells glistening with some delectable sauce, appears at the banquet table. How are they to attack the crab? There is no way to avoid messy fingers, ricocheting shells, sauce dripping from chins, and a history of the dish recorded on clothes. While Asians love spending an hour leisurely picking every fragment of crabmeat from the shell, Americans often just make a cursory attack at the crab before impatiently rushing on to the next dishes. This recipe answers those frustrations by using fresh lump crabmeat or soft-shell crabs. If using soft-shell crabs, ask the fishmonger to clean them for you, and cook them the day that you buy them.

ADVANCE PREPARATION

Cut soft-shell crabs into quarters; refrigerate. If using lump crabmeat, pick through and remove any shell or cartilage; refrigerate. Cut the mushrooms into ¹/₄-inch slices. Seed, stem, and sliver the red pepper and refrigerate with the mushrooms. Keep basil and sprouts refrigerated (do not wash). Combine the ginger, garlic, lemongrass, if using, butter, and oil. Combine all the sauce ingredients in a bowl, stir well, and refrigerate. *Can be completed to this point up to 8 hours in advance of Last-Minute Cooking.*

LAST-MINUTE COOKING

Place a sauté pan or wok over highest heat and add the ginger-butter mixture. When the butter bubbles and the seasonings sizzle, about 1 minute, add the soft-shell crabs, if using. Sauté over highest heat until the crabs turns red, about 2 minutes. Add the mushrooms and pepper. Sauté over high heat until the pepper brightens, about 30 seconds.

If using lump crabmeat, add it now, along with the basil, sprouts, and sauce. Cook until the sauce comes to a low boil and thickens slightly. Serve at once.

MENU IDEAS: For two, serve this with a spinach salad, rice pilaf, a fine white wine, and a dessert from Chapter 7.

Serves: 2 as an entrée.

Asian Barbecued Salmon

1 salmon fillet with skin,
  approximately 2 pounds
2 tablespoons flavorless
  cooking oil
Lemon wedges

MARINADE
¼ cup Chinese rice wine or
  dry sherry
¼ cup light soy sauce
2 tablespoon oyster sauce
2 tablespoons fresh lemon juice
2 tablespoons dark sesame oil
½ teaspoon freshly ground
  black pepper
1 bunch chives, minced
¼ cup finely minced ginger

This dish recalls the memory of the grilled fish served at the huge Palm Beach Restaurant, located inside Singapore's modern National Sports Stadium. On a warm night filled with gentle trade winds and the chatter of cicadas, we pushed our way through the crowds at the entrance and crossed the huge dining room to the circular tables next to a floor-to-ceiling glass wall looking out onto the soccer field. As their national team practiced just feet away, eight hundred enthusiastic Singaporeans consumed platters of chile crab, lo hay raw fish salads, crunchy fried squid, crisp dumpling purses filled with shellfish, and barbecued pomfret served on banana leaves. Little children pounded the crabs with metal mallets, toothless grandmothers slurped fish soup, a staff of seventy rushed from table to kitchen, and we fantasized about converting "Dodger Dogs" and the press box at Chavez Ravine into a similar restaurant. This is one of the easiest recipes in the book. If you wish to broil the fish, have the salmon skinned, and then broil the fillet 3 inches from the heat for approximately 10 minutes.

PREPARATION AND COOKING

Remove any stray bones from the fillet using tweezers or needle-nose pliers, then transfer the salmon to a nonreactive bowl. Set aside the cooking oil and lemon wedges separately. Combine all the marinade ingredients and mix well. Add the marinade to the salmon, turning the salmon over to cover. Marinate for 15 minutes to 2 hours. *Can be completed to this point up to 2 hours in advance of Last-Minute Cooking.*

LAST-MINUTE COOKING

If using a gas barbecue, heat to medium (350°F). If using charcoal or wood, prepare the fire. When the coals or wood are ash-covered, brush the barbecue rack with the cooking oil, and lay the salmon on top, skin side down. Immediately cover and cook the salmon until it just begins to flake, about 12 minutes. (If the barbecue cannot be covered, place the salmon in a wire fish basket and turn the salmon once during cooking; total cooking time will be about 18 minutes.) During cooking, brush the salmon with the marinade.

Carefully slide a spatula under the fillet and transfer to a heated serving platter. The spatula will slide easily between the flesh and the skin (the skin remains on the grill). For a large fillet, two people will be needed to transfer the fish to the serving platter. Serve immediately with lemon wedges.

MENU IDEAS: Quick outdoor dinner for four—Asian Barbecued Salmon served with pasta seasoned with olive oil, salt, pepper, and Parmesan; a simple green salad; and berries with store-bought ice cream.

Serves: 4 as an entrée.

Crisp Panfried Trout

2 fresh trout, 8 ounces each
  (preferably with bone in)
2 green onions, white and
  green parts
¼ cup cornstarch
½ cup flavorless cooking oil

SAUCE
1 tablespoon finely minced
  ginger
½ cup chicken broth
2 tablespoons Chinese rice
  wine or dry sherry
2 tablespoons oyster sauce
2 teaspoons cornstarch
½ teaspoon sugar
¼ teaspoon freshly ground
  black pepper

This is an excellent example of a dish best suited for a small dinner party. Count on serving one small trout per person, perhaps with an Asian salad and a rice dish. Since a twelve-inch sauté pan accommodates three eight-ounce trout, you can triple the recipe and simultaneously cook enough trout in two skillets for an informal dinner, while five friends gather in the kitchen to enjoy a glass of wine and watch the crisp trout skin pick up the beautiful glaze of the sauce.

ADVANCE PREPARATION

Keep trout refrigerated. Mince the green onions and refrigerate. Set aside the ¼ cup cornstarch and the cooking oil separately. Set aside the ginger for the sauce. In a small bowl, combine the remaining sauce ingredients, stir well, and refrigerate. *Can be completed to this point up to 8 hours in advance of Last-Minute Cooking.*

LAST-MINUTE COOKING

Place the trout on a layer of newspaper or a baking sheet. Dust the trout on both sides with ¼ cup cornstarch, shaking the trout to remove any excess. Place a heavy 12-inch skillet over medium-high heat. When very hot, add the oil. When the oil becomes very hot (it should appear thinner and give off a little haze), add the trout. Shake the pan to prevent the trout skin from sticking, and panfry for about 3 minutes on each side, regulating the heat so the oil always sizzles but does not smoke. The trout are cooked when the end of a chopstick easily sinks into the flesh.

Temporarily remove the trout to a layer of paper toweling. Discard the oil from the frying pan, then return the pan to medium-high heat. Add minced ginger and green onions. When the green onions brighten, add the sauce and bring to a boil. Immediately return the trout to the pan and turn them over in the sauce. Transfer the trout and sauce to a heated platter or plates. Serve at once.

MENU IDEAS: This would be delicious served with Champagne Rice Pilaf (page 143) and a tomato-and-avocado salad, and for dessert, vanilla-bean ice cream and Chocolate Mudslide Cookies (page 165).

Serves: 2 as an entrée.

Smoked Rib-Eye Steaks with Ginger-Mango Salsa

4 rib-eye steaks, 10 ounces each,
  trimmed of fat
Barbecue Sauce from Smoked
  Baby Back Ribs (page 105) or
  Mesquite Barbecued Lamb
  (page 107)
1 cup wood chips (any kind)

GINGER-MANGO SALSA
2 small ripe mangoes, 1 papaya,
  or 4 peaches
2 tablespoons minced green
  onion, white and green parts
1/4 cup minced cilantro sprigs
1/2 cup finely minced ginger
3 tablespoons fresh lime juice
2 tablespoons brown sugar
2 tablespoons Thai or
  Vietnamese fish sauce
1 teaspoon Asian chile sauce

Everyone will have far more fun at home parties if the cook matches a simple menu with recipes using easy preparation techniques and cooking methods. Let restaurant chefs slave in their kitchens doing impossible recipes while the rest of us serve simple foods with glorious tastes that cause spirits to soar. The menu for an easy Father's Day dinner might be Crazy Caesar Salad; Smoked Rib-Eye Steaks with Ginger-Mango Salsa (Dad does the barbecuing) accompanied by sautéed baby carrots, snow peas, and red pepper; New Wave Garlic Bread; and, for dessert, Raspberry Cabernet Sauvignon Tart.

ADVANCE PREPARATION

Rub the steaks with the barbecue sauce and marinate for at least 15 minutes but not longer than 4 hours. Set aside wood chips. To prepare the salsa, peel the mango, cut flesh off into large pieces, and finely chop. If using papaya, peel, cut in half, scoop out the seeds, and chop flesh; if using peaches, drop in boiling water for 20 seconds, plunge in cold water, then pit, seed, and chop. Transfer fruit to a bowl, add remaining ingredients, stir well, and refrigerate. *Can be prepared to this point up to 4 hours in advance of Last-Minute Cooking.*

LAST-MINUTE COOKING

Soak the wood chips in water for 30 minutes before using. Bring salsa to room temperature. If using a gas barbecue, heat to medium (350°F). If using charcoal or wood, prepare the fire. When the coals or wood are ash-covered, drain the chips and place them on a 6-inch square of aluminum foil, directly on the coals. When the wood begins to smoke, brush the rack with oil, lay the ribs on top, and cover the barbecue. Cook for about 5 minutes on each side for medium-rare. Alternatively, broil the steaks for about 4 minutes on each side. Transfer to warmed dinner plates, spoon the salsa next to each steak, and serve at once.

Serves: 4 as an entrée.

Smoked Rib-Eye Steaks with Ginger-Mango Salsa

Barbecued Veal Chops with Macadamia Nuts

Barbecued Veal Chops with Macadamia Nuts

4 veal chops, 10 ounces each
2 ounces toasted macadamia
  nuts

MARINADE
4 cloves garlic, finely minced
1 tablespoon finely minced
  ginger
1 tablespoon grated or finely
  minced lemon zest
1 tablespoon grated or finely
  minced orange zest
1/4 cup minced chives, basil
  leaves, or cilantro sprigs
1/3 cup fresh lemon juice
1/4 cup fresh orange juice
3 tablespoons Chinese rice wine
  or dry sherry
3 tablespoons extra-virgin
  olive oil
3 tablespoons oyster sauce
2 tablespoons Dijon mustard
1/2 teaspoon Asian chile sauce

This recipe uses one of our favorite marinades. Its blend of lemon, orange, Dijon mustard, and oyster sauce is an ideal flavor combination for marinating veal, pork, chicken, or fish in preparation for barbecuing. It is also an excellent marinade-basting sauce for sliced eggplant, large strips of peppers, and portobello mushrooms. Marinate the vegetables for only 20 minutes, or the eggplant and mushrooms will become mushy. Then grill the vegetables until they soften and acquire a slightly charred exterior.

ADVANCE PREPARATION

Place the chops in a single layer in a nonreactive dish and refrigerate. If the nuts are salted, rinse with cold water, then pat dry. Coarsely chop the macadamia nuts with a knife (not in the food processor). Combine all the marinade ingredients in a bowl, stir well, and refrigerate. *Can be completed to this point up to 8 hours in advance of Last-Minute Cooking.*

LAST-MINUTE COOKING

At least 15 minutes but not longer than 2 hours before cooking, pour the marinade over the chops and turn them to coat evenly. If using a gas barbecue, heat to medium (350°F). If using charcoal or wood, prepare fire. When the coals or wood are ash-covered, brush the grilling rack with oil, and place the chops on the grill, reserving the excess marinade. Grill the veal for about 10 minutes on each side, basting with some of the reserved marinade. The veal is done when the internal temperature reaches 150°F and the meat feels firm when pressed with your fingers. Alternatively, broil the chops for about 5 minutes on each side.

   Place the chops on dinner plates. Transfer the marinade to a small saucepan, bring to a boil, and spoon it over the chops. Sprinkle the macadamia nuts on top. Serve at once.

MENU IDEAS: Labor Day dinner for ten without the labor! Begin with large chilled, cooked shrimp accompanied by two Pacific Flavors dipping sauces; follow with Barbecued Veal Chops with Macadamia Nuts (triple the recipe) served with Champagne Rice Pilaf (page 143; double the recipe, cook ahead, and reheat in the oven or microwave); and for the grand finale, have Mango Ice Cream (page 157) with a hot fudge sauce.

Serves: 4 as an entrée.

Sichuan Veal Meat Loaf

Tropical Fruit Salsa (page 39) or
  Ginger Mango Salsa (page 94)
1 cup pine nuts
2 pounds ground veal
2 slices white bread, or 1/2 cup
  unseasoned bread crumbs
1/2 cup chopped onions
5 cloves garlic, finely minced
1 tablespoon grated or finely
  minced tangerine zest
2 large eggs
1/2 cup ketchup
2 tablespoons oyster sauce
1 tablespoon Asian chile sauce

It is so much fun to add an Asian accent to a traditional American favorite such as meat loaf. Standard Asian ingredients that perk up American food include mint, tangerine zest, ginger, fish sauce, coconut milk, soy sauce, oyster sauce, hoisin sauce, sesame oil, and Asian chile sauce. Give your most conservative houseguests a hint of Pacific flavors by serving Tex-Mex Wontons, then spoonfuls of Tropical Fruit Salsa on thick slabs of Sichuan Veal Meat Loaf, accompanied by Crazy Coconut Noodle Toss and a finale of Orange Ginger Brownies with a premium store-bought ice cream. Your guests' palates will be forever transformed.

ADVANCE PREPARATION

Prepare a salsa, and refrigerate. Heat the oven to 325°F. Spread pine nuts on a baking sheet and toast until golden, about 10 minutes. Place the veal in a large bowl; add the pine nuts. Trim and discard the crusts from bread. Put the bread in a food processor, mince until finely crumbled, and add to the veal. Add all the remaining ingredients. Mix gently with your fingers until evenly combined, but do not overmix, or the meat loaf will have a very dense texture. Gently pack into a 9-by-5-inch loaf pan and refrigerate. *Can be completed to this point up to 8 hours in advance of Last-Minute Cooking.*

LAST-MINUTE COOKING

Bring the salsa and meat loaf to room temperature. Heat the oven to 400°F. Bake meat loaf until it is piping hot, about 30 minutes. Slice and serve with the salsa of your choice.

Serves: 4 to 6 as an entrée.

Chiu Chow Lemon Chicken

8 chicken breast halves (about
    4 ounces each), boned
    and skinned
1 cup slivered almonds
1 bunch chives
4 cloves garlic, finely minced
1 tablespoon finely minced
    ginger

SAUCE
2 teaspoons grated or finely
    minced lemon zest
1/2 cup fresh lemon juice
6 tablespoons sugar
1/4 cup chicken broth, preferably
    homemade (page 69)
2 tablespoons light soy sauce
1 tablespoon cornstarch
1/2 teaspoon salt

TO FINISH
1/4 cup flavorless cooking oil
Salt and freshly ground black
    pepper
1 cup all-purpose flour
2 tablespoons unsalted butter

Platters laden with chilled cracked crab, thinly sliced soy goose, double-boiled duck soup with salt lemon; an expressway noise volume from nine hundred fellow diners; chefs in the display kitchen cleaving steamed lobster; Jim Beam whiskey enriching a soup at a neighboring table; fried sliced pomfret; and Tsing Tao beer contribute to a kaleidoscope of impressions at City Chiu Chow Restaurant in Hong Kong. This recipe adapts one of the restaurant's dishes by using the sauce for pan-fried chicken breasts. You can also drizzle the sauce over barbecued chicken or grilled swordfish, or use it as a dip for chilled cooked jumbo shrimp.

ADVANCE PREPARATION

Trim all fat from chicken, then refrigerate. Heat oven to 325°. Spread almonds on a baking sheet and toast until light golden; set aside. Mince the chives and set aside. Combine the garlic and ginger and set aside. Combine the sauce ingredients in a small bowl and mix well; refrigerate. *Can be complete to this point up to 8 hours in advance of Last-Minute Cooking.*

LAST-MINUTE COOKING

Place a small nonreactive saucepan over medium heat. Add 1 tablespoon cooking oil and then the garlic and ginger. Sauté briefly, then add the sauce. Bring to a low boil and reduce to a simmer.

Sprinkle the chicken on both sides with a little salt and pepper. Dust with flour, shaking off any excess. Place a 14-inch skillet over high heat or use two smaller skillets at the same time. When hot, add the butter and remaining 3 tablespoons of oil. When the butter bubbles, add all the chicken pieces to the skillet(s), making sure that none of the pieces overlap. Cook for about 2 minutes on each side. The chicken is done when the meat loses its raw color in the interior (cut into a piece) and feels firm to the touch. Transfer the chicken to a heated platter or dinner plates.

Spoon the sauce over the chicken. Sprinkle the almonds and chives on top. Serve at once.

Serves: 4 as an entrée.

Roast Chicken with Zinfandel Mushroom Sauce

2 chickens, about 3 pounds
   each, cut into 6 to 8 pieces
5 tablespoons unsalted butter

ZINFANDEL MUSHROOM SAUCE
5^{1}/$_{3}$ tablespoons unsalted butter
2 small yellow onions, minced
4 cloves garlic, finely minced
1^{1}/$_{2}$ pounds mushrooms
   (portobello, shiitake,
   button), stems discarded,
   cut into ^{1}/$_{4}$-inch-wide slices
1 cup red wine, such as
   Zinfandel
1 cup chicken broth
2 tablespoons oyster sauce
1 tablespoon dark soy sauce
2 teaspoons tomato paste
^{1}/$_{2}$ teaspoon Asian chile sauce
^{1}/$_{2}$ teaspoon sugar
1 tablespoon chopped fresh
   thyme leaves
1 tablespoon cornstarch
Salt and freshly ground black
   pepper

The key technique in this recipe is to roast the chicken on an elevated rack so that the hot oven air circulates around the chicken and causes the skin to become crisp. On the other hand, if you lay the chicken pieces on the surface of a shallow-edged baking sheet, the chicken steams on the bottom and will acquire a pale, anemic look when fully cooked. This recipe pairs roast chicken with one of our favorite sauces. The sauce can be made entirely ahead of time and only needs to be reheated. As an alternative cooking method for the chicken, rub it with the marinade from Barbecued Veal Chops with Macadamia Nuts, marinate for 15 minutes, and then grill. Roast Chicken with Zinfandel Mushroom Sauce, little boiling potatoes, and a spinach salad with a vinaigrette would be a perfect weekend dinner.

ADVANCE PREPARATION

Rinse, dry, and refrigerate chicken pieces. Set aside the 5 tablespoons butter. Prepare mushroom sauce: Have ready the butter, onion, and garlic. Combine all remaining ingredients in a bowl.

Place a 12-inch nonreactive sauté pan over medium heat. Melt half the butter and add the onions; sauté until they become golden, about 15 minutes. Add the remaining butter, and when it melts, add the garlic and mushrooms. Sauté mushrooms until they expel their moisture, wilt, and become densely textured, about 15 minutes. Add the wine mixture and set aside if using within 1 hour, or refrigerate. *Can be completed to this point up to 8 hours in advance of Last-Minute Cooking.*

LAST-MINUTE COOKING

Heat the oven to 425°F. Elevate a flat rack on the edges of a baking sheet (some wire racks have their own legs), place the chicken on the elevated rack, dot with butter, and place the baking sheet in the oven. Roast for 30 to 40 minutes, basting every 10 minutes with the pan juices. The chicken is done when the internal temperature reaches 160°F for the breast pieces and 170°F for the legs and thighs, and the juices are no longer tinged with pink when the chicken is pierced deeply.

Bring the mushroom sauce to a boil over high heat and cook until the sauce thickens, about 5 minutes. Taste and adjust seasonings. Place the mushroom sauce on a heated serving platter or dinner plates, add the chicken pieces, and serve at once.

Serves: 4 as an entrée.

Southern Fried Chicken, Pacific-style

2 cups buttermilk or milk
½ cup chopped fresh basil leaves
½ cup chopped cilantro sprigs
2 green onions, white and green parts, minced
4 cloves garlic, finely minced
2 tablespoons finely minced ginger
2 tablespoons white sesame seeds, toasted
1 tablespoon red-pepper flakes
1 tablespoon salt
1 chicken, about 3 pounds, cut into pieces
3 cups all-purpose flour
2 cups flavorless cooking oil

Golden fried chicken, southern style, with its moist meat and a crisp exterior speckled with fresh herbs, garlic, and chiles, sets off dramatic explosions of contrasting flavors and textures with each bite. The chicken is coated with batter ahead of time so that the batter dries and thus adheres better during cooking. The chicken does require careful attention during the last-minute frying, so keep the accompanying dishes simple. We like to serve the chicken with a dipping sauce such as Tropical Fruit Salsa (page 39), New Age Guacamole (page 42), or Peanut Satay Sauce (page 41), and accompany it with California Cornbread, a salad of tossed greens, and homemade apple pie.

ADVANCE PREPARATION

In a large bowl, combine the buttermilk or milk, basil, cilantro, green onions, garlic, ginger, sesame seeds, red-pepper flakes, and salt. Stir well. Add the chicken and marinate in the refrigerator for 8 hours. *Must be completed to this point 8 hours in advance of Last-Minute Cooking.*

LAST-MINUTE COOKING

Place the flour in a large bowl. Roll the chicken pieces one at a time in the flour, then shake off excess flour and transfer to a wire rack placed on a baking sheet. Refrigerate the chicken pieces on the wire rack, uncovered, for at least 45 minutes or as long as 6 hours.

Place the cooking oil in a deep 12-inch skillet over medium-high heat, and heat to 365°F (bubbles will come out from the end of a wooden spoon when oil is ready). Place the chicken skin side down in the hot oil. Reduce the heat to medium, and fry the chicken until golden on one side (about 10 minutes). Turn the pieces and cook until golden on the other side (about 10 minutes more). Turn the chicken pieces again and cook for about 5 minutes more. During cooking, adjust the heat so the oil is always bubbling around the pieces but is never smoking. The chicken is done when the internal temperature reaches 165°F, or when the juices run clear when the chicken is pierced deeply with a fork. Drain the chicken on paper towels. Transfer to a heated platter or dinner plates and serve at once.

Serves: 4 as an entrée.

Thai-High Barbecued Chicken

2 frying chickens, about 3½ pounds each, split in half

MARINADE
6 cloves garlic, minced
1 tablespoon minced ginger
4–8 small hot chiles (preferably serrano), minced including seeds
4 whole small green onions, white and green parts, minced
¼ cup minced cilantro sprigs
1 tablespoon grated or minced lime zest
Juice from 2 limes
¼ cup hoisin sauce
¼ cup red wine vinegar
¼ cup Thai or Vietnamese fish sauce
¼ cup honey
2 tablespoons dark soy sauce
2 tablespoons flavorless cooking oil

Near the White Reclining Buddha in Ayuthaya, the ancient capital of Thailand, is a courtyard of large stone Buddhas, all draped with saffron robes, who witness perspiring tourists climbing steep stairs to the top of the ruins. Skinny temple dogs and laughing children play by an old bull and dart past wooden signs inscribed with Buddhist sayings such as Victory Begets Revenge. At the temple entrance, barefoot cooks barbecue chicken on small, open, elevated rectangular pits of wood coals. The chicken, flavored with garlic, fresh chiles, and lime, provides a strengthening mid-morning snack before we explore more ruins.

ADVANCE PREPARATION

Working with one chicken half, loosen a small area of the skin along the top of the breast. Gently push your index finger underneath the skin, moving it along the breast, thigh, and drumstick and being careful not to dislodge the skin attached to the backbone. Repeat with the remaining chicken halves.

Combine all the marinade ingredients in a bowl and stir well. Spoon about one-eighth of the marinade under the skin of each chicken half and, with your fingers, massage the outside of the skin to work the marinade over the breast, thigh, and drumstick. Rub another eighth of the marinade over the entire outside surface of each chicken half. Refrigerate for at least 30 minutes and not longer than 8 hours. *Can be completed to this point up to 8 hours in advance of Last-Minute Cooking.*

LAST-MINUTE COOKING

Pour any remaining marinade into a small saucepan and bring to a boil for 1 minute, then reserve. If using a gas barbecue, heat to medium (350°F). If using charcoal or wood, prepare a fire. When the coals or wood are ash-covered, brush the grill rack with oil, then grill the chicken halves over medium heat for about 30 minutes, or until a meat thermometer reads 170°F when plunged deep into a chicken thigh. When pierced with a fork, the juices should run clear. Or roast the chicken halves meat side up in a 425°F oven for about 30 minutes.

Serve the chicken with the reserved marinade. Spoon a little of the sauce over the chicken for added flavor. The chicken is excellent eaten hot, at room temperature, or cold with the reserved marinade. If you wield a Chinese cleaver with great dexterity, chop the chicken into bite-size pieces before serving cold, as part of a picnic.

Serves: 4 as an entrée.

Smoked Baby Back Ribs with Pacific Flavors Barbecue Sauce

4 slabs baby pork back ribs,
   each with 6 ribs (about 1³/₄
   pounds total)
2 cups wood chips

PACIFIC FLAVORS BARBECUE
SAUCE
1 tablespoon chopped garlic
1 tablespoon finely minced
   ginger
¹/₄ cup minced green onions,
   white and green parts
¹/₄ cup minced cilantro sprigs
2 teaspoons grated or finely
   minced orange zest
¹/₂ cup hoisin sauce
¹/₃ cup plum sauce
2 tablespoons dark sesame oil
2 tablespoons white vinegar
2 tablespoons oyster sauce
2 tablespoons dark soy sauce
2 tablespoons honey
2 tablespoons Chinese rice wine
   or dry sherry
2 teaspoons Asian chile sauce

Giving barbecued meat a smoky flavor is so easy and adds a complex taste. Among the many wood chips sold at gourmet shops and home-improvement centers are maple, cherry, hickory, mesquite, and our favorite, oak-barrel staves from wine barrels. Just soak the chips for thirty minutes, drain, and place on a layer of aluminum foil directly on the coals. When the chips begin to smoke, barbecue the meat or seafood. Keep the barbecue top closed during cooking to intensify the smoky flavor.

The barbecue sauce lasts indefinitely in the refrigerator if you omit the green onions and cilantro (their fresh taste quickly deteriorates). We give cooking friends this barbecue sauce packaged in jars labeled: "Good on all meats and seafood that you barbecue, broil, or roast." The first time you try this recipe, serve it with corn on the cob, parsley potatoes, and lemon meringue pie.

ADVANCE PREPARATION

On the underside of the ribs is a tough white membrane; using your fingernail or a sharp, pointed knife, loosen the membrane along the bone at one edge, then, gripping the membrane with a paper towel, pull it away and discard. Refrigerate ribs. Set aside the wood chips. Combine all the barbecue-sauce ingredients in a bowl, stir well, and refrigerate. Makes 1½ cups. *Can be completed to this point up to 8 hours in advance of Last-Minute Cooking.*

LAST-MINUTE COOKING

Soak the wood chips in water for 30 minutes before using. Rub the ribs with barbecue sauce and marinate for no more than 30 minutes. If using a gas barbecue, heat to medium (350°F). If using charcoal or wood, prepare a fire. When the coals or wood are ash-covered, drain the chips and place them on a 6-inch square of aluminum directly on the coals. When the chips begin to smoke, brush the rack with oil, lay the ribs on top, and cover the barbecue. Cook until the meat begins to shrink away from the ends of the rib bones, about 45 to 60 minutes. Brush the ribs with more barbecue sauce halfway through cooking. Or, alternatively, to roast the ribs, place them meaty side up on a flat elevated rack placed on a baking sheet, place in a 350° oven, and roast until the meat begins to shrink from the ends of the bones, about 1 hour. Serve hot or at room temperature. If eating the ribs as an appetizer, cut into individual ribs before serving them.

Serves: 12 as an appetizer or 4 as an entrée.

*Smoked Baby Back Ribs with
Pacific Flavors Barbecue Sauce and
Asian Noodle Magic (recipe on page 138)*

Beef Tenderloin with Thai Green Curry Sauce

3 pounds beef tenderloin, trimmed
Marinade from Mesquite Barbecued Lamb (page 107)

SAUCE
1/2 cup chicken broth, preferably homemade (page 69)
2 tablespoons Thai or Vietnamese fish sauce
2 whole cloves
8 whole black peppercorns
1 teaspoon coriander seeds
1/2 teaspoon caraway seeds
1/2 teaspoon cumin seeds
3 cloves garlic, peeled
1 small shallot, peeled
4 whole fresh serrano chiles, stemmed
1/2 cup fresh basil leaves, loosely packed
1/3 cup cilantro sprigs
1/4 cup mint leaves
2 tablespoons flavorless cooking oil

Beef tenderloin makes a great party dish. It takes only a few minutes to combine the marinade, and then only occasional supervision while the beef sizzles on the grill. The beef in this recipe would be very good just sliced and served with mashed potatoes infused with garlic. But when the beef is placed on a complexly flavored Thai green curry sauce and accompanied by a rice pilaf from this book, the combination of colors, flavors, and textures transforms the very good to the sublime. Ask your butcher to trim all the fat and silver skin from the outside of the beef, and if the meat is from the fat end of the loin, to cut the meat into its individual muscles. It's better to have to cook several small pieces, rather than one large piece, so everyone can have meat cooked to his individual preference.

ADVANCE PREPARATION

Combine the marinade ingredients in a nonreactive dish large enough to hold the beef. Add beef and rub the marinade over its surface. Marinate for at least 15 minutes but no longer than 8 hours, refrigerated.

Prepare the sauce: Combine the chicken broth and fish sauce, and refrigerate. Place the cloves, peppercorns, coriander, caraway, cumin, and salt in a small sauté pan; set over high heat and toast until the spices just begin to smoke, about 1 minute. Immediately transfer to a spice grinder and grind until completely powdered. In a food processor, finely mince the garlic, shallots, and chiles. Add the herbs and ground spices and finely mince. With the machine on, slowly pour the oil down the feed tube of the food processor. Process into a paste; transfer to a small container, cover with plastic wrap, and refrigerate. *Can be completed to this point up to 8 hours in advance of Last-Minute Cooking.*

LAST-MINUTE COOKING

Bring the meat to room temperature. If using a gas barbecue, heat to medium (350°F). If using charcoal or wood, prepare a fire. When the coals or wood are ash-covered, brush the grill with oil, lay the beef on top, and cover the barbecue. Cook, occasionally brushing on more marinade and turning the beef over. The beef is done when the internal temperature reaches 140°F on a meat thermometer, about 20 minutes. Or, place the beef on a elevated wire rack over a baking sheet and roast in a 500°F oven for approximately 20 minutes.

Remove the meat from the grill and let rest for 5 minutes. In the meantime, place a 10-inch sauté pan over medium-high heat. Add green curry paste and sauté for 30 seconds, then stir the chicken broth mixture and add it to the sauté pan. Bring the sauce to a low boil, stirring. Taste and adjust the seasonings. Cut the beef into 6 steaks. Place a steak on each dinner plate. Drizzle sauce over the meat and serve at once.

Serves: 6 as an entrée.

Mesquite Barbecued Lamb with Asian Seasonings

1 leg of lamb, about 5 pounds,
   boned and butterflied
2 cups mesquite or other
   wood chips

BARBECUE SAUCE
1 cup hoisin sauce
¾ cup plum sauce
¼ cup white vinegar
¼ cup Chinese rice wine or
   dry sherry
3 tablespoons honey
2 tablespoons dark soy sauce
2 tablespoons dark sesame oil
1 tablespoon Asian chile sauce
8 cloves garlic, finely minced
1 tablespoon grated or finely
   minced orange zest

ACCOMPANIMENTS
8 cups shredded salad greens
4 cups shredded carrots (about
   3 large carrots)
2 cups cilantro sprigs
2 cups fresh mint leaves
1 cup fresh basil leaves
Tropical Fruit Salsa (page 39)
Double recipe of Peking Chive
   Pancakes (page 150) or
   about 40 flour tortillas

This is one of our favorite party recipes. The lamb is butterflied, marinated, and then smoked over wood chips. Once cooked, the lamb is sliced and accompanied by small plates containing herbs, salsa, and hot Peking Chive Pancakes or flour tortillas. Each person opens a pancake, adds a slice of meat, a sprinkling of greens and carrots, and a choice of fresh herbs, then drizzles on the salsa and rolls the pancake into a cylinder to eat. It's a marvelously informal way to dine, immensely satisfying to even the most jaded palate, and always generates a high degree of enthusiasm with all those present.

ADVANCE PREPARATION

Trim off all fat from the outside of the lamb. Set aside the chips. In a nonreactive dish large enough to hold the lamb, combine all the ingredients for the barbecue sauce and mix well. Add lamb and marinate in the refrigerator for at least 15 minutes but not longer than for 4 hours. Prepare the accompaniments. Enclose the pancakes or tortillas in an airtight aluminum package, and refrigerate. *Can be prepared to this point up to 4 hours in advance of Last-Minute Cooking.*

LAST-MINUTE COOKING

Bring the lamb to room temperature. Soak the wood chips for 30 minutes. If using a gas barbecue, heat to medium (350°F). If using charcoal or wood, prepare a fire. When the coals or wood are ash-covered, drain the chips and place on a 6-inch square of aluminum directly on the coals. When the chips begin to smoke, brush the barbecue rack with oil and lay the lamb flat on top. Turn the lamb over every 5 to 8 minutes, basting it with the barbecue sauce as it cooks. The lamb is done when the temperature on a meat thermometer reaches 140°F for medium-rare or 160°F for medium (30 to 45 minutes). Or, alternatively, roast the lamb in a 450°F oven 20 to 30 minutes.

    Heat the oven to 325° for warming the wrappers. Place the greens, carrots, and herbs on separate serving plates or on one large platter. Have the salsa nearby. Heat the pancakes or tortillas for 15 minutes, then transfer to a basket lined with a cloth napkin; fold the napkin over the top and bring to the table. Remove the meat from the grill and bring to the table. Thinly slice the lamb and serve with the accompanying herbs, salsa, and pancakes.

Serves: 10 as an entrée.

Spicy Chicken with Lettuce Cups

CHAPTER 5

Mu Shu Fantasies and Stir-Fry Triumphs

Stir-frying is a rhythmical dance, a swirl of action in a softly curved pan, a flash of motion as the surface sizzles and alluring aromas capture the attention of all present. No other cooking technique lends itself better to improvisation, speedy preparation steps, and astonishingly quick cooking. No other technique produces such succulent meats, crunchy vegetables, and beautifully glazed foods.

Test out this theory by stir-frying shrimp with chiles and orange zest—or clams in a Singapore curry sauce—and accompany them with steamed Thai jasmine rice. Flash-cook ground beef, lots of garlic, and chiles, and use this as a stuffing for a Pacific-style burrito or to place on pasta just removed from the boiling water. Another night, sear marinated bay scallops in a blazing wok and slide them onto a dinner salad to produce a quick workday dinner. Or stir-fry thinly sliced pork tenderloin marinated with a little hoisin sauce and dark sesame oil, place in hot corn or flour tortillas along with spoonfuls of a spicy store-bought salsa, and roll these into cylinders and eat using your fingers. Accompanied by a simple salad dressed with oil and vinegar, or perhaps a side dish from the following chapter, any of the recipes in this chapter will make you return to stir-frying night after night.

Use this chapter as your stir-fry primer. Read through the paragraphs introducing the recipes and review the principles for stir-frying on pages 170–171. Perfect your wok technique by making the following recipes, and then become the best stir-fry artist in your neighborhood. Home cooking will never be the same.

Spicy Chicken with Lettuce Cups

1 pound boneless chicken breast halves, trimmed of all fat
1 tablespoon dark soy sauce
1 tablespoon Chinese rice wine or dry sherry
2 teaspoons dark sesame oil
4 green onions, white and green parts
2 small zucchini
4 cloves garlic, finely minced
2 teaspoons finely minced ginger
2 heads endive or Bibb lettuce
3 tablespoons flavorless cooking oil

SAUCE
1/2 cup unsweetened coconut milk
3 tablespoons Chinese rice wine or dry sherry
2 tablespoons Thai or Vietnamese fish sauce
1 tablespoon hoisin sauce
2 teaspoons curry powder
2 teaspoon cornstarch
1 teaspoon Asian chile sauce
1/2 cup chopped fresh mint leaves
1/4 cup chopped fresh basil leaves

Imagine serving this or another favorite stir-fry cradled in lettuce as an appetizer, or as the opening course for dinner. Since the recipe requires last-minute cooking, follow this course with other Pacific flavors or American fare already completed and ready to be brought straight from the kitchen. A good menu from this book would be to start the dinner by serving Firecracker Dumplings, then stir-fry this dish and serve with Asian Polenta, followed by Pacific Flavors Salad, and for dessert, a store-bought ice cream topped with Raspberry Cabernet Sauvignon Sauce.

ADVANCE PREPARATION

Cut the chicken into 1/4-inch cubes; add the soy sauce, rice wine, and sesame oil, stir to combine, and refrigerate. Cut the green onions on the diagonal into 1/4-inch pieces. Cut the zucchini on a sharp diagonal into 1/4-inch-thick slices; overlap the slices and cut into 1/4-inch-thick strips, then cut across the strips to cube. Combine green onions and zucchini; refrigerate. Combine garlic and ginger. Separate endive or lettuce leaves into cups and refrigerate. Set aside cooking oil. Combine all the sauce ingredients in a small bowl, then refrigerate. *Can be completed to this point up to 8 hours in advance of Last-Minute Cooking.*

LAST-MINUTE COOKING

Stir the sauce. Place the wok over highest heat. When the wok is very hot, add 2 tablespoons of the cooking oil to the center. Tilt the wok to coat the sides with oil. When the oil just begins to smoke, add the chicken and stir-fry until it just loses it raw outside color, about 1 minute. Transfer to a platter.

Immediately return the wok to highest heat. Add the remaining 1 tablespoon oil to the center, then add the garlic mixture. Sauté for a few seconds, then add the vegetables. Stir-fry until the onions brighten, about 2 minutes. Return the chicken to the wok and pour in the sauce. When the sauce comes to a low boil, taste and adjust the seasonings. Transfer to a heated platter or dinner plates. Serve at once with the lettuce cups. Each person puts some of the filling in a lettuce cup, gently cups the edges, and eats it quickly!

Serves: 8 as an appetizer, or 2 to 4 as an entrée.

Stir-Fried Shrimp with Garlic and Chiles

1 pound large raw shrimp,
  in the shell
2 tablespoons flavorless
  cooking oil
4 cloves garlic, finely minced
1 tablespoon finely minced
  ginger
2 teaspoons grated or finely
  minced orange zest
4 small chiles, stemmed and
  minced
Chinese rice wine or dry sherry
  to taste
Dark sesame oil to taste
Pinch of sugar

If you stir-fry shrimp in their shells, the shrimp will be more tender and the flavor of the shells will intensify the taste. However, if you don't want messy hands, shell the shrimp in advance of cooking and be sure not to overcook them. Use the seasoning mix of garlic, chiles, and sesame oil as a starting point and create your own flavor variation. Add one tablespoon of hoisin sauce, or a quarter cup chopped cilantro, mint, or basil, or replace the fresh chiles with a half teaspoon or more of your favorite chile sauce. For an easy dinner, accompany this dish with a tossed green salad. Or serve the shrimp chilled, as an appetizer.

ADVANCE PREPARATION

Using scissors or a thin knife, cut along the top of the shrimp shell to expose the vein. Rinse out the vein, being careful to keep the shell intact; refrigerate. (If you shell the shrimp, cut them deeply along the top so that they are nearly split in half.) Combine the oil, garlic, ginger, orange peel, and chiles. *Can be completed to this point up to 8 hours in advance of Last-Minute Cooking.*

LAST-MINUTE COOKING

Place the wok over highest heat. When very hot, add the oil mixture and sauté for a few seconds. Add the shrimp and stir and toss until the shells turn pink (a few black scorch marks are fine). The shrimp are cooked when they feel firm to the touch. Or cut one in half; it should be white in the center. During the last minute of cooking, add a splash of rice wine or sherry, drizzle the sesame oil on top, and add the sugar. Taste and adjust the seasonings. Transfer to a heated platter or plates. Serve hot, at room temperature, or cold. Each person peels off the shells at the table.

Serves: 6 to 8 as an appetizer, or 3 as an entrée.

Scallops and Cashews in Tangerine Sauce

Scallops and Cashews in Tangerine Sauce

2 cups raw cashews
2 cups flavorless cooking oil
4 green onions, white and green parts, chopped
4 cloves garlic, finely minced
1 pound fresh bay scallops

SAUCE
1/4 cup Chinese rice wine or dry sherry
3 tablespoons tomato sauce
1 tablespoon oyster sauce
1 tablespoon dark sesame oil
2 teaspoons cornstarch
1 teaspoon red wine vinegar
1/2 teaspoon Asian chile sauce
2 teaspoons grated or finely minced tangerine or orange zest

Giving scallops, thinly sliced filet mignon, or shrimp a brief stir-fry in a blazing wok, with a splash of sauce added to glaze the food, is the easiest, most practical way to stir-fry at home. This means no hours of cutting up different types of exotic Asian vegetables, no frantic relays of food in and out of the wok, no exhaustion! Meat or seafood, stir-fried and rolled in hot flour tortillas, or placed on a snow-white bed of deep-fried rice sticks, or cupped in crisp lettuce pockets, makes a satisfying and quick entrée.

ADVANCE PREPARATION

Place the nuts and oil in a small saucepan over medium-high heat. Stir occasionally, and when nuts turn very light golden, drain immediately and pat dry on paper towels. Pour off the oil, reserving 2 tablespoons for stir-frying. Cool and discard remaining oil. Set aside and refrigerate in separate containers the green onions, garlic, and scallops. Combine the sauce ingredients in a small bowl, mix well, and refrigerate. *Can be completed to this point up to 8 hours in advance of Last-Minute Cooking.*

LAST-MINUTE COOKING

Stir the sauce. Place a wok over highest heat. When the wok is very hot, add the reserved oil to the center. Roll the oil around the sides of wok and add the garlic. When it just begins to turn white, about 15 seconds, add the scallops. Stir-fry until the scallops just lose their raw outside color, about 1 minute.

Stir in the green onions and pour in the sauce. When the sauce comes to a low boil, stir in the cashews, then taste and adjust the seasonings. Spoon onto a heated platter or individual plates. Serve at once.

MENU IDEAS: A work-night dinner for two—Scallops and Cashews in Tangerine Sauce served with steamed jasmine rice, an avocado-and-papaya salad, and fresh fruit.

Serves: 4 as an entrée.

Curried Clams with Basil and Cilantro

26 small steamer clams
2 tablespoons cornmeal
3 cloves garlic, finely minced
1 tablespoon finely minced ginger
2 tablespoons flavorless cooking oil

SAUCE
1/2 cup total any combination of minced fresh basil, mint, and cilantro
3/4 cup unsweetened coconut milk
1/4 cup tomato sauce
1/4 cup Chinese rice wine or dry sherry
2 tablespoons oyster sauce
1 tablespoon curry powder
1 tablespoon dark sesame oil
2 teaspoons cornstarch
1 teaspoon Asian chile sauce
1/2 teaspoon sugar

At an eating paradise in Singapore, the famous outdoor hawkers' food mall at Newton Centre, friends feast on chile crab, oyster omelets, crackling deep-fried squid, and crunchy pan-fried noodles cooked in a huge wok by a wizened Chinese lady. Another round of beer promises new forays to other food stalls for huge barbecued prawns, spicy coconut chicken soup, and courageous tastings of the stinky durian fruit. Gentle trade winds blow and hawkers shout their triumphs, such as this dish of curried clams. For your own outdoor party on a hot summer night, start with chilled shrimp with one of the Pacific Flavors Dipping Sauces, then curried clams served with Champagne Rice Pilaf, a salad of mixed greens and ripe papaya, and, for dessert, Lemon Ice Cream with Chocolate Grand Marnier Sauce.

ADVANCE PREPARATION

Scrub the clams. Cover with cold water and stir in the cornmeal to make the clams spit out any sand. After 1 hour, discard any clams that are not tightly closed. Drain, rinse, and refrigerate until ready to use. Combine and set aside the garlic, ginger, and cooking oil. Combine the sauce ingredients in a small bowl and refrigerate. *Can be completed to this point up to 8 hours in advance of Last-Minute Cooking.*

LAST-MINUTE COOKING

Stir the sauce. Place a colander inside a larger bowl near the stove. Have ready a fine-mesh sieve. Place a wok over high heat, and when hot, add 1 cup hot water. When the water comes to a boil, add the clams and cover the wok. When all the clams open, 3 to 5 minutes, tip the clams into the colander, reserving the steaming liquid in the bowl. Discard any clams that do not open.

Return the wok to highest heat. When hot, add the oil mixture. Sauté until the garlic begins to sizzle but has not turned brown. Add the sauce. Bring the sauce to a low boil. Return the clams to the wok. Pour half the steaming liquid through the sieve into the wok. Toss the clams until they are evenly glazed with the sauce. Transfer to a platter and serve at once.

Serves: 2 as an entrée.

Flower Blossom Squid

1½ pounds small squid
½ red bell pepper, seeded
¼ cup chopped fresh basil,
    mint, or cilantro
3 cloves garlic, finely minced
3 small chiles, minced
1 tablespoon grated or finely
    minced lime zest
¼ cup chicken broth, preferably
    homemade (page 69)
¼ cup light brown sugar
¼ cup white vinegar
1 tablespoon Thai or
    Vietnamese fish sauce
2 ounces rice sticks
2 cups flavorless cooking oil
1 tablespoon cornstarch

The key technique in cooking squid is to cook it fast! Because many home stoves do not generate very high heat, stir-fried squid will often expel its moisture and steam to a rubbery toughness. For all stir-fry squid recipes, do the following: After stir-frying the vegetables and adding the sauce to the wok, immerse the squid in a large amount of rapidly boiling water. In five seconds the squid will turn white and be fully cooked. Immediately tip the squid into a colander, and then (moving fast!) transfer the squid to the wok. Give the vegetables, squid, and sauce a quick stir to evenly glaze all ingredients, and then transfer to a heated platter or dinner plates. Cooked in this manner, the squid will be very tender.

ADVANCE PREPARATION

Clean the squid: Pull the head from the squid and cut the tentacles off in one piece. If the black mouth is in the center of the tentacles, pull this away and discard. Discard the rest of the head. Under cold running water, rub off the squid skin with your fingers. Run a thin knife inside the squid and open into a flat steak. Clean inside thoroughly. Making light lengthwise cuts, score the inside of the squid in a crisscross pattern, being careful not to cut all the way through. Cut each steak into quarters and refrigerate along with the tentacles.

Chop the red pepper. Refrigerate the pepper and the herbs. In a small bowl, combine the garlic, chiles, lime zest, broth, brown sugar, vinegar, and fish sauce; refrigerate. Deep-fry the rice sticks in the cooking oil as described on page 46. *Can be completed to this point up to 8 hours in advance of Last-Minute Cooking.*

LAST-MINUTE COOKING

Break the rice sticks into small pieces and place in a thin layer on a serving platter or four dinner plates. Combine the cornstarch with an equal amount of cold water and set aside. In a large pot, bring 5 quarts of water to a rapid boil.

Place the wok over high heat, add the sauce, and bring to a rapid boil. Stir occasionally. When the sauce turns a caramel color, about 8 minutes, stir the squid into the boiling water. As soon as the squid turns white, about 10 seconds, drain in a colander; shake the colander vigorously to thoroughly drain all the water. Immediately transfer the squid to the wok. Stir in the red pepper and herbs. Add a little cornstarch mixture to lightly thicken the sauce so squid pieces are glazed. Turn out onto rice sticks and serve at once.

MENU IDEAS: This dish is great served with Peanut Ginger Noodle Salad (page 56), Three Mushroom Soup (page 81), and a peach tart for dessert.

Serves: 2 to 4 as an entrée.

OVERLEAF: *Flower Blossom Squid on Rice Sticks*

Spicy Stir-Fry Beef

1 pound beef tenderloin or other
  tender cut of boneless meat
2 tablespoons flavorless
  cooking oil

ALL-PURPOSE STIR-FRY
MARINADE
2 tablespoons Chinese rice wine
  or dry sherry
1 tablespoon hoisin sauce
1 tablespoon oyster sauce
1 tablespoon dark sesame oil
$\frac{1}{2}$ teaspoon Asian chile sauce
$\frac{1}{2}$ teaspoon finely minced or
  grated orange zest
3 cloves garlic, finely minced
1 green onion, white and green
  parts, finely minced

This recipe provides a marinade and a stir-fry technique that we frequently use. The marinade is great for any tender cut of meat such as chicken breasts, pork tenderloin, boneless leg of lamb, and beef tenderloin. The amount is sufficient for one-half to one pound of meat. Marinate the meat for 15 minutes to 1 hour. Stir-fried in a very hot wok, the meat tastes great slid onto dinner salads that have been lightly dressed with an oil-and-vinegar dressing, or accompanied by warm pita bread, or placed on top of eight ounces of boiled and drained fusilli.

ADVANCE PREPARATION

Trim off all fat from the outside of the meat. Cut the meat across the grain into $\frac{1}{4}$-inch slices. Cut the slices into $\frac{1}{2}$-inch-wide rectangles or into matchstick-shaped pieces, place in a bowl, and refrigerate. Set aside the cooking oil. Combine all the marinade ingredients in a small bowl and stir well; refrigerate. *Can be completed to this point up to 8 hours in advance of Last-Minute Cooking.*

LAST-MINUTE COOKING

Pour the marinade over the beef, and use your fingers to mix evenly. Marinate for 15 minutes to 1 hour. Place a wok over highest heat. When the wok becomes very hot, add the cooking oil to the center. Roll the oil around the wok, and when the oil just gives off a wisp of smoke, add the beef. Stir and toss the beef until it loses all of its raw outside color, about 2 minutes. Immediately slide the beef onto a heated plate. Place the beef on top of a dinner salad, accompany by heated tortillas, or serve with steamed white rice.

Serves: 2 as an entrée.

Thai Pork Tenderloin with Sweet Peppers

1 pound pork tenderloin, trimmed of fat
2 tablespoons Chinese rice wine or dry sherry
2 tablespoons hoisin sauce
1 each red, green, and yellow bell pepper
4 green onions, white and green parts
3 cloves garlic, finely minced
1 tablespoon finely minced ginger

SAUCE
3 tablespoons chopped fresh basil leaves
3 tablespoons chopped cilantro sprigs
1/2 cup unsweetened coconut milk
1/4 cup Chinese rice wine or dry sherry
1/4 cup tomato sauce
2 tablespoons oyster sauce
1 tablespoon cornstarch
1/2 teaspoon Asian chile sauce

3 tablespoons flavorless cooking oil

A key stir-fry principle is to stir-fry the meat or seafood separately from the vegetables so that each ingredient is perfectly cooked and to avoid overloading the wok with food. Meat or seafood is always stir-fried first, then temporarily set aside while the vegetables are stir-fried, and then returned to the wok for a few brief moments. It's important not to overcook the meat or seafood during the preliminary cooking. Always transfer the meat (even if it's pork) or seafood from the wok while the pieces are still undercooked in the center. The meat or seafood will continue to cook while it rests on the plate, and when it is returned to the wok, the very high heat quickly finishes the cooking process.

ADVANCE PREPARATION

Cut the pork in half lengthwise; place halves together and cut them crosswise into 1/8-inch-wide pieces. Transfer to a bowl, mix evenly with the rice wine and hoisin sauce, and refrigerate. Seed, stem, and cut the peppers into 1/2-inch cubes. Cut the green onion on a diagonal into 1-inch pieces. Combine the peppers and green onions and refrigerate. Combine the garlic and ginger. In a bowl, combine the sauce ingredients, stir well, and refrigerate. *Can be completed to this point up to 8 hours in advance of Last-Minute Cooking.*

LAST-MINUTE COOKING

Place a wok over highest heat. When the wok becomes very hot, add 2 tablespoons of the cooking oil to the center. Roll the oil around the wok, and when the oil just gives off a wisp of smoke, add the pork. Stir and toss the pork until it loses its raw outside color, about 2 minutes. Slide the pork onto a plate.

Immediately return the wok to the burner over highest heat. Add the remaining 1 tablespoon cooking oil and the ginger and garlic and stir-fry. As soon as they turn white, about 5 seconds, add the vegetables. Stir and toss until the green onions turn a brighter green, about 1 minute.

Stir the sauce, and then pour into the wok. Return the pork to the wok. Stir and toss until all the ingredients are glazed with the sauce. Taste and adjust the seasonings. Immediately transfer the stir-fry to a heated platter or dinner plates and serve at once.

MENU IDEAS: Serve this with steamed jasmine rice, one of the salads from Chapter 2, and Lemon Ice Cream (page 159).

Serves: 4 as an entrée.

Asian Lamb Wraps

1 pound boneless leg of lamb,
    trimmed of all fat
1 tablespoon hoisin sauce
2 teaspoons dark soy sauce
2 tablespoons plus 2 teaspoons
    flavorless cooking oil
1 red bell pepper
3 green onions, white and green
    parts
4 cloves garlic, finely minced

SAUCE
3 tablespoons Chinese rice wine
    or dry sherry
2 tablespoons hoisin sauce
1 tablespoon dark soy sauce
1 tablespoon dark sesame oil
2 teaspoons cornstarch
2 teaspoons red wine vinegar
1 teaspoon Asian chile sauce
1/4 teaspoon sugar
1/4 teaspoon salt

TO FINISH
Tropical Fruit Salsa (page 39) or
    New Age Guacamole
    (page 42)
8 eight-inch flour tortillas

If you are using only a very small amount of quick-cooking vegetables (less than 2 cups), as here, add the vegetables to the meat or seafood the moment it loses its raw outside color. As the meat or seafood is stir-fried for a few more seconds, the small amount of vegetables will brighten and become fully cooked. This recipe would be great served with a salad of baby lettuce greens lightly dressed with oil and vinegar, and perhaps preceded by one of the dumpling recipes from Chapter 1.

ADVANCE PREPARATION

Cut the lamb into 1/8-inch slices, then cut the slices into very thin slivers. Place the meat in a bowl and mix in the hoisin sauce, soy sauce, and the 2 teaspoons cooking oil; refrigerate. Stem, seed, and cut the pepper into 1-inch-long slivers. Cut the green onions into the same-length slivers. Combine the vegetables and refrigerate. Mince the garlic and set aside. Combine the sauce ingredients in a small bowl and mix well. Prepare the salsa or guacamole. *Can be completed to this point up to 8 hours in advance of Last-Minute Cooking.*

LAST-MINUTE COOKING

Place the salsa or guacamole in a decorative bowl. Wrap the tortillas in foil and heat for 8 minutes in a 350°F oven. Place a wok over highest heat. When the wok is very hot, add the remaining 2 tablespoons cooking oil and the garlic. Tilt the wok to coat the sides with the oil. When the garlic just begins to turn white, in about 15 seconds, add the lamb. Stir-fry until the lamb just loses its raw outside color, about 1 minute.

Add the vegetables. Pour in the sauce and bring to a boil. Taste and adjust the seasonings, then spoon onto a heated platter or individual plates. Serve with the salsa or guacamole and hot flour tortillas.

Serves: 4 as an entrée.

Asian Lamb Wraps with New Age Guacamole, Tropical Fruit Salsa, and the Mexican rice drink horchata

Sichuanese Chicken with Eggplant

1 pound boneless, skinless
   chicken breasts
All-Purpose Marinade (page 118)
1 yellow onion
4 small Japanese eggplants or 1
   large eggplant
1 tablespoon cornstarch
3 tablespoons flavorless
   cooking oil

SAUCE
$^1/_3$ cup chicken broth
3 tablespoons Chinese rice wine
   or dry sherry
2 tablespoons oyster sauce
1 tablespoon hoisin sauce
1 tablespoon red wine vinegar
1 tablespoon dark sesame oil
1 teaspoon sugar
1 teaspoon Asian chile sauce
$^1/_4$ cup chopped cilantro sprigs

Eggplant is one of the few vegetables that needs to be covered and steam-cooked in the wok. Once the eggplant is briefly stirred and tossed in the hot wok, any stir-fry sauce in this chapter can be added, and the wok covered. During the few minutes that it takes for the eggplant to soften and lose its raw taste, the top is periodically removed and the eggplant is given a quick toss with the sauce. This recipe is very good with the chicken eliminated and the eggplant served as a vegetable side dish accompanying barbecued meat. Or replace the sauce with the coconut-curry-herb sauce on page 85.

ADVANCE PREPARATION

Cut the chicken breasts into inch-wide strips. Cut across the strips into $^1/_4$-inch-wide slices. In a bowl, combine the chicken with the marinade, mix well, and refrigerate. Peel the onion and cut into $^1/_2$-inch cubes. Discard the eggplant stems. Cut the Japanese eggplants in half lengthwise; then cut across the eggplants, making $^1/_4$-inch-wide slices. If using 1 large eggplant, cut into $^1/_2$-inch-wide strips, then cut across the strips into $^1/_4$-inch-wide slices. Combine the vegetables and refrigerate. Set aside the cornstarch and oil in separate containers. Combine the sauce ingredients and refrigerate. *Can be completed to this point up to 8 hours in advance of Last-Minute Cooking.*

LAST-MINUTE COOKING

Combine the cornstarch with an equal amount of cold water. Place a wok over the highest heat. When the wok becomes very hot, add 1 tablespoon of the oil. Roll the oil around the wok and when the oil gives off just a wisp of smoke, add the chicken. Stir and toss until the chicken just loses its raw outside color. Immediately transfer the chicken to a plate.

   Return the wok to highest heat. Add the rest of the cooking oil, rolling it around the sides of the wok. Add the vegetables. Stir and toss until the vegetables begin to sizzle in the pan. Stir the sauce and then pour it into the wok. Cover the wok and steam the vegetables; periodically remove the cover, stir the vegetables, and re-cover. Continue to steam until the eggplant softens, about 4 minutes.

   When the eggplant become soft, return the chicken to the wok. Add a little of the cornstarch mixture so that the sauce thickens slightly. Stir and toss for a few seconds, and then immediately transfer to a heated platter or dinner plates. Serve at once.

Serves: 4 as an entrée.

Mu Shu Pork Bonanza

1 pork tenderloin, trimmed of
   all fat
2 tablespoons hoisin sauce, plus
   more for serving
2 tablespoons Chinese rice wine
   or dry sherry
4 ounces fresh shiitake
   mushrooms
2 zucchini
4 green onions, white and green
   parts
4 large eggs, well beaten
3 cloves garlic, minced
5 tablespoons flavorless
   cooking oil

SAUCE
3 tablespoons Chinese rice wine
   or dry sherry
1 tablespoon dark soy sauce
1 tablespoon oyster sauce
2 teaspoon cornstarch
$\frac{1}{2}$ teaspoon freshly ground
   black pepper

12 Peking Chive Pancakes
   (page 150)

Mu Shu is the most popular Chinese restaurant dish in the United States. Tender Peking pancakes, crunchy shredded vegetables, succulent meat, and accents of hoisin sauce create a taste bonanza. Since the Peking Chive Pancakes freeze well, make them far ahead of the event. This dish is just as good when you replace the pork with shredded chicken, beef tenderloin, lamb, or a mix of fresh shiitake mushrooms, thin asparagus, and green onions. If you don't want to make the pancakes, substitute flour tortillas or frozen mu shu wrappers sold at Asian markets. Serve this dish as the entrée for four people, followed by a salad course.

ADVANCE PREPARATION

Cut the meat crosswise into $\frac{1}{8}$-inch slices, stack the slices, and cut into 2-inch slivers. Combine the meat with the 2 tablespoons hoisin sauce and rice wine; mix well and refrigerate. Discard mushroom stems and cut mushrooms caps into slivers. Cut zucchini and green onions into slivers. Combine the vegetables and refrigerate. Refrigerate the eggs. In separate containers set aside the garlic and cooking oil. In a small bowl, combine the sauce ingredients. Prepare (or thaw) the pancakes. *Can be completed to this point up to 8 hours in advance of Last-Minute Cooking.*

LAST-MINUTE COOKING

Heat the oven to 325°. Wrap the pancakes in aluminum foil and heat for 15 minutes. Place a wok over highest heat. When the wok is very hot, add 2 tablespoons of oil to the center. Tilt the wok to coat the sides with oil. When the oil just begins to smoke, add the pork. Stir and toss until the pork just loses its outside color; then slide the pork onto a platter.

Immediately return the wok to highest heat. Add 1 tablespoon of the cooking oil, rolling it around the sides of the wok, then add the eggs. Scramble the eggs until they become firm, about 1 minute. Slide the eggs onto the pork.

Immediately return the wok to highest heat. Add the remaining 2 tablespoons oil to the center, then add the garlic. Sauté for a few seconds, then add the vegetables, stir-frying until the green onions brighten, about 1 minute. Return the pork and eggs to the wok, then stir the sauce and add it to the wok. Taste and adjust the seasonings. Tip the food onto a heated platter. Serve with the hot pancakes and a dish of hoisin sauce. Each person spreads a little hoisin sauce across the center of the pancake, places about $\frac{1}{2}$ cup filling on top of the sauce, then rolls the pancake into a cylinder, folding the bottom end upward to keep the filling from escaping. Filled pancakes are eaten with the fingers.

Serves: 4 as an entrée.

Spicy Chicken Wraps

Meat from one Thai-High
  Barbecued Chicken
  (page 103)
¼ cup Thai-High Marinade that
  never came into contact with
  the raw chicken
½ hothouse cucumber
2 bunches cilantro sprigs
Tropical Fruit Salsa (page 39) or
  Ginger-Mango Salsa
  (page 94)
12 taco shells or soft flour or
  corn tortillas
1 tablespoon flavorless
  cooking oil

Leftover meat or seafood briefly stir-fried in a searingly hot wok makes a quick and flavor-intense entrée. Try replacing any of the raw meat or seafood used in this chapter with already cooked meat or seafood. Cut the meat or seafood into thin slices, then stir-fry the vegetables, add the sauce, and when the sauce glazes the vegetables, stir in the meat or seafood. Cook until just heated through, and serve. Try serving this dish as part of a "South of the Border" party theme. With a mariachi band playing, serve Tex-Mex Wontons with New-Age Guacamole, Tex-Mex Salad, Spicy Chicken Wraps accompanied with California Cornbread with plenty of sweet butter and wild clover honey, and Mango Ice Cream. Don't forget the margaritas!

ADVANCE PREPARATION

Cut the meat and crisp skin from the barbecued chicken into shreds and refrigerate until ready to use. Set aside the marinade. Cut the cucumber on a sharp diagonal into ¼-inch slices. Stack the slices and cut into shreds. Set aside. Wash and thoroughly dry the cilantro. Set aside. Prepare the salsa. If using soft tortillas, wrap air-tight with aluminum foil and refrigerate. *Can be completed to this point up to 8 hours in advance of Last-Minute Assembling.*

LAST-MINUTE ASSEMBLING

Heat the oven to 325°F. Place the soft tortillas in the oven for 15 minutes, until piping hot. Place a wok over highest heat. When piping hot, add the oil. Roll the oil around the sides. When it gives off a wisp of smoke, add the chicken. Stir and toss until the chicken becomes hot. Add the marinade and toss briefly. Transfer the chicken to a platter. Accompany with the taco shells or tortillas, cucumber, salsa, and cilantro. Each person assembles the tacos, first placing a layer of chicken in the bottom of the shell, followed by layers of salsa, cucumber, and a few cilantro sprigs.

Serves: 2 to 4 people as an entrée.

Spicy Chicken Wraps with Ginger-Mango Salsa

Spicy Orange Lamb with Peppers and Onions

1 pound ground lamb or other
　meat
All-Purpose Marinade
　(page 118)
2 yellow onions
1 each red, green, and yellow
　bell pepper
3 tablespoons flavorless
　cooking oil

Sauce
3 tablespoons chicken broth
2 tablespoons Chinese rice wine
　or dry sherry
2 tablespoons oyster sauce
1 tablespoon hoisin sauce
1 tablespoon dark sesame oil
1 tablespoon curry powder
1 teaspoon Asian chile sauce
1 teaspoon cornstarch
1 tablespoon finely minced
　ginger
1 teaspoon finely minced or
　grated orange zest

Raw ground lamb, beef, and pork taste wonderful when stir-fried. They can replace any of the meat or seafood used in this chapter. Mix the raw ground meat with the All-Purpose Marinade from page 118, and let marinate for a minimum of five minutes but not longer than eight hours. As you stir-fry the ground meat, press it with the back of a flat wooden spatula so that it separates into individual grounds. The following recipe is one my Chinese friends and I cooked often in college.

ADVANCE PREPARATION

Combine the meat with the marinade in a bowl, mix well, and refrigerate. Peel and cut the onion into 1/2-inch cubes. Seed, stem, and cut peppers into 1/2-inch cubes. Combine the vegetables and refrigerate. Set aside the cooking oil. Combine the sauce ingredients in a bowl and refrigerate. *Can be completed to this point up to 8 hours in advance of Last-Minute Cooking.*

LAST-MINUTE COOKING

Place the wok over highest heat. When hot, add half the oil to the center. Tilt the wok to coat the sides with oil. When the oil just begins to smoke, add the meat. Stir-fry, pressing meat against the sides of the wok, until it loses all of its raw color and breaks apart into little grains, about 5 minutes. Transfer to a plate.

　　Immediately return the wok to highest heat. Add the remaining oil to the center, then add the vegetables. Stir and toss until the onions lose their raw color and the peppers brighten, about 2 minutes.

　　Return the meat to the wok. Stir the sauce and pour it into the wok. Stir and toss until the sauce glazes the food. Taste and adjust the seasonings. Transfer to a heated serving platter or dinner plates. Serve at once.

Menu Ideas: Serve with steamed jasmine rice and a simple dinner salad.

Serves: 4 as an entrée.

Shrimp in Black Bean Sauce

1 pound large raw shrimp
1 bunch asparagus
1 yellow zucchini
3 green onions, white and green parts
2 tablespoons finely minced ginger
3 cloves garlic, finely minced
1 tablespoon salted black beans
1 large egg, well beaten
3 tablespoons flavorless cooking oil

SAUCE
1/3 cup chicken broth, preferably homemade (page 69)
3 tablespoons Chinese rice wine or dry sherry
2 tablespoons light soy sauce
1 tablespoon dark sesame oil
1 teaspoon sugar
1/2 teaspoon Asian chile sauce
12 bamboo skewers, 4 to 6 inches long
1 pound skinless, center-cut salmon fillet
Pacific Flavors Dipping Sauces (pages 40–43) of your choice

SALMON-GRILLING MARINADE
3 tablespoons fresh lime juice
3 tablespoons flavorless cooking oil
3 tablespoons light brown sugar
2 tablespoons Thai or Vietnamese fish sauce or light soy sauce
1 teaspoon Asian chile sauce
2 tablespoons very finely minced ginger
3 tablespoons minced cilantro sprigs

Shrimp in black-bean sauce is a classic Cantonese dish. It gains its flavor from salted, fermented black beans, which are very pungent. We find that bottled black-bean sauces, such as the Lee Kum Kee brand available at Asian markets, are so salty that even the addition of a tiny amount ruins the food. We prefer the salted black beans to the bottled sauces. The best are sold in yellow cardboard canisters and say on the label Yang Jiang Preserved Beans with Ginger, Pearl River Bridge brand. To use, rinse and chop coarsely.

ADVANCE PREPARATION

Shell, devein, and split the shrimp in half and refrigerate. Snap off and discard the tough asparagus ends. Cut the asparagus on a sharp diagonal, giving the spear a quarter turn after each cut. Cut the zucchini in half lengthwise and then into four long strips. Cut the strips diagonally into 1-inch lengths. Cut the green onions on a sharp diagonal into 1-inch pieces. Combine the vegetables and refrigerate. Combine the ginger and garlic. Rinse the black beans briefly with cold water, press out excess, chop finely, and add to the ginger. Refrigerate the egg. Set aside the oil. Combine the sauce ingredients in a bowl, and refrigerate. *Can be completed to this point up to 8 hours in advance of Last-Minute Cooking.*

LAST-MINUTE COOKING

Stir the sauce. Place a wok over highest heat. When very hot, add half the oil to the center of the wok. Roll the oil around the sides of the wok. When the oil begins to smoke, add the shrimp and stir-fry until it just loses its raw outside color, about 1 minute. Transfer to a platter.

Immediately return the wok to high heat. Add the remaining oil and the ginger-black bean mixture. Stir-fry for a few seconds and then add the vegetables. Stir and toss until the vegetables brighten, about 2 minutes.

Add the sauce and cook until it forms a glaze around the food. Turn off the heat, drizzle the beaten egg over the shrimp, and cover the wok until the egg cooks, about 30 seconds. Taste and adjust seasonings. Slide the shrimp onto a heated platter or dinner plates and serve at once.

MENU IDEAS: Serve with Asian Polenta (page 131), one of the salads from Chapter 2, and Raspberry Cabernet Sauvignon Tart (page 160).

Serves: 2 to 4 as an entrée.

Barbecued Vegetables with Pacific Flavors

CHAPTER 6

Magical Side Dishes for Any Entrée

The many easy recipes in this chapter are good examples of our passion for serving food that has lots of flavor. Whether it is a simple vegetable stir-fry, crisp grilled vegetables brushed during cooking with Asian seasonings, or stir-fried noodles glazed in a coconut-basil sauce, each recipe is a rainbow of exciting texture, color, and flavor contrasts. As you cook, taste, taste, and taste again. Fingers dip into sauces, the pepper grinder rattles over a bubbling soup, hands move quickly to chop extra basil, and a dash of oyster sauce provides that sought-after rich flavor. Danny Kaye was fond of saying, "If you give ten people the same recipe, ten different dishes always result." Cooking is not a science, and even a cook who has just discovered that room called "the kitchen" can add a new culinary chapter with dramatic last-minute seasoning additions. The results may not be perfect, but these spontaneous personal touches make cooking an adventure and create magic for the table.

Barbecued Vegetables with Pacific Flavors

VEGETABLES

1 pound (4–6 cups) asparagus, broccoli, carrots, cauliflower, eggplant, green beans, green onions, mushrooms, peppers, summer squash

VEGETABLE BARBECUE SAUCE

1/4 cup minced green onions (white and green parts), fresh basil, or cilantro sprigs

1 tablespoon finely minced ginger

3 cloves garlic, finely minced

1 tablespoon grated or finely minced lemon zest

1/3 cup fresh lemon juice

3 tablespoons Chinese rice wine or dry sherry

3 tablespoons extra-virgin olive oil

2 tablespoons light soy sauce

1/4 teaspoon freshly ground black pepper

Barbecued vegetables taste sensational! Serve them hot or chilled as appetizers, add them to salads, take them straight from the barbecue and roll them in heated flour tortillas with added spoonfuls of Ginger-Mango Salsa (page 94), or use them as a bold-tasting vegetable accompaniment to meat and seafood entrées.

Choose vegetables that lie flat on the barbecue and are large enough not to fall through the grill. Longer-cooking vegetables, such as broccoli and cauliflower, should be blanched first, and then barbecued just long enough to pick up the wonderful smoky taste.

The following recipe gives a simple olive oil, lemon, and soy sauce barbecue sauce to brush across the vegetables as they cook. But for a different flavor try the marinades from Barbecued Veal Chops with Macadamia Nuts (page 97) or Asian Barbecued Salmon (page 92).

PREPARATION

Bring 4 quarts of water to a boil. Prepare your choice of vegetables: Snap off the tough bottoms of asparagus stems. Cut the broccoli, including some of the stems, into long pieces, then drop into boiling water and cook until the color brightens; transfer immediately to ice water, chill, and pat dry. Peel the carrots; if large, split in half lengthwise. Cut the cauliflower into long pieces and blanch for 2 minutes. Cut the eggplant into 1/2-inch slices. Cut off the stems from the green beans. Discard the root ends and ragged green tips from the green onions. Trim the tough stems from mushrooms. Stem and seed the peppers; cut into 2-inch-wide strips. Trim the stem end from the squash, then cut into long 1/2-inch-thick pieces. After all the vegetables are blanched, refrigerate them.

Combine all the ingredients for the sauce in small bowl and mix well; refrigerate. *Can be completed to this point up to 8 hours in advance of Last-Minute Cooking.*

BARBECUING VEGETABLES

If using a gas barbecue, heat to medium (350°F). If using charcoal or wood, prepare the fire. When the coals or wood are ash-covered, brush the vegetables with the sauce and place on the grill. Barbecue the vegetables until they are tender, turning them over occasionally and brushing them with more of the barbecue sauce.

Serves: 4 to 6 as a side dish.

Asian Polenta

2 cups yellow cornmeal
2 teaspoons salt
2 cloves garlic, minced
2 tablespoons finely minced ginger
1 teaspoon finely minced or grated orange zest
8 tablespoons (1 stick) unsalted butter
½ cup freshly grated imported Parmesan
1 tablespoon extra-virgin olive oil

This is a perfect side dish to serve with any of the entrées in this book. The polenta, subtly perfumed with ginger and grated orange, is cooked far in advance, and takes only minutes to reheat under the broiler. We particularly like serving it as the side dish to stir-frys. If you want more assertive flavors and textures, try adding one or any combination of the following, stirring them in at the same time you add the butter: ⅓ cup toasted pine nuts, ½ cup dried currants, ½ cup chopped roasted red pepper, ¼ cup chopped fresh cilantro, 1 cup raw kernels from white sweet corn, and ½ teaspoon Asian chile sauce.

ADVANCE PREPARATION

In a large saucepan, combine 6 cups water, the cornmeal, salt, garlic, ginger, and orange zest. Place over high heat and bring to a low boil, stirring frequently. As the mixture begins to thicken, reduce the heat to low. Stir the polenta until it becomes very thick and the cornmeal no longer tastes raw, about 15 minutes from the time the water comes to a boil. Stir in the butter and cheese. As soon as the butter melts and is evenly incorporated into the mixture, tip the polenta onto a shallow baking sheet. Using a rubber spatula, spread the polenta into a ½-inch layer. Let polenta cool and become firm, then cut into serving-size pieces, such as 3-inch squares, rectangles, or circles. Refrigerate the polenta uncovered. *Can be completed to this point up to 8 hours in advance of Last-Minute Cooking.*

LAST-MINUTE COOKING

Turn the oven setting to broil. Rub the olive oil over the surface of the polenta, place it four inches below the broiler heat, and broil until browned and thoroughly heated, about 8 minutes. Using a flexible metal spatula, transfer the polenta to heated dinner plates. Serve at once.

Serves: 4 to 8 as a side dish.

Crazy Coconut Noodle Toss

½ pound dried spaghetti-style
  noodles
3 tablespoons flavorless
  cooking oil
1 cup thinly sliced fresh button
  mushrooms
1 red bell pepper, seeded and
  slivered
1 cup slivered red cabbage
  (about ¼ cabbage)
1 cup stemmed and slivered
  snow peas

SAUCE
¾ cup unsweetened coconut
  milk
2 tablespoons Chinese rice wine
  or dry sherry
1 tablespoon oyster sauce
1 tablespoon light soy sauce
2 teaspoons cornstarch
1 teaspoon Asian chile sauce
¼ teaspoon salt
¼ cup chopped fresh basil
  leaves
⅓ cup chopped fresh mint
  leaves
⅓ cup chopped green onions,
  white and green parts

This recipe, one of our signature dishes, is easy to vary. Try using other types of noodles, such as fettuccine, or the shorter pastas, such as penne or rotelle. Substitute fresh shiitake mushrooms for the button mushrooms; use a different fresh herb blend, such as a mix of mint, cilantro, and basil, or use just one kind of herb. Add one teaspoon of curry powder to the coconut sauce, or half a cup of seeded and finely minced vine-ripened tomatoes. Transform this dish into an entrée by stir-frying one pound of raw shelled shrimp until they turn white on the outside. Set the shrimp aside while you complete the cooking steps, and return them at the end. If you have access to fresh crabmeat, stir it into the noodle dish during the last moments of cooking. Whatever variations you try, the resulting fresh flavors will create an exciting merging of Thai, Chinese, and contemporary American cooking styles that is bound to impress your guests.

ADVANCE PREPARATION

Bring 4 quarts of water to a rapid boil and drop in the noodles. Cook until they lose their raw taste but are still firm, about 5 minutes. Drain, rinse with cold water, and drain again. Toss the noodles with 1 tablespoon of the cooking oil and set aside. Prepare the vegetables. Toss the noodles and vegetables together in a bowl and refrigerate. Combine the sauce ingredients in a small bowl and refrigerate. *Can be completed to this point up to 8 hours in advance of Last-Minute Cooking.*

LAST-MINUTE COOKING

Place a wok or skillet over highest heat. Add the remaining 2 tablespoons of cooking oil. When very hot, add the noodle mixture. Sauté for about 3 minutes, until the noodles begin to heat.

Add the sauce and bring to a low boil. Stir and toss until the noodles are well heated. Taste and adjust the seasonings. Transfer to a heated platter or to individual plates. Serve at once.

MENU IDEAS: A quick family meal—broiled fish, Crazy Coconut Noodle Toss, and a tossed green salad.

Serves: 4 as a pasta side dish with any meat or seafood entrée.

Hot Potatoes Two Ways

2½ pounds russet potatoes
  (about 5)
8 tablespoons (1 stick) unsalted
  butter
5 cloves garlic, finely minced
½ cup half-and-half
¼ cup prepared horseradish
1 teaspoon salt

Mashed potatoes go very well with many of the entrées in this book. This recipe provides two ways to make them. If serving the mashed potatoes within one hour, transfer them to a metal container and place the container in simmering water. This will keep the potatoes piping hot. But mashed potatoes are just as good made hours in advance and reheated: Transfer them to a baking dish and refrigerate. When ready to serve, reheat the potatoes in a 350° oven until piping hot, and then broil them until lightly browned. Our other favorite method for cooking potatoes is to rub fingerling or small red potatoes with olive oil, minced garlic, salt, and pepper, and oven-roast at 450° until the potatoes are tender when stabbed deeply with a fork. All these methods produce potatoes that are great served with any of the meat or seafood entrées in Chapter 4.

ADVANCE PREPARATION

Peel the potatoes. Cut each potato into 4 pieces and transfer to a large saucepan filled with a generous amount of cold water, so that the potatoes are completely covered. Bring the water to a boil, reduce the heat to low, and cook the potatoes at a low boil until they become tender, about 20 minutes. Immediately drain, then return potatoes to the hot saucepan.

Meanwhile, place the butter and garlic in a small saucepan over low heat. Melt the butter; remove the saucepan from the heat when the garlic begins to sizzle but has not begun to brown. In a microwave oven or in a saucepan, warm the half-and-half. While the potatoes are still piping hot, mash them with a potato masher or the tongs of a fork. Add the butter, garlic, half-and-half, and horseradish. Stir to evenly combine. Add salt to taste (about 1 teaspoon). If serving the potatoes within 1 hour, transfer them to a small, metal container. Place the container inside a large saucepan of simmering water over medium-low heat. If making the potatoes further ahead, place them in a small ovenproof dish, cover with plastic wrap, and refrigerate. *Can be completed to this point up to 8 hours in advance of Last-Minute Cooking.*

LAST-MINUTE COOKING

If the mashed potatoes are being kept warm in the simmering water bath, serve within 1 hour. If the mashed potatoes have been transferred to an ovenproof dish, heat the oven to 350°F. Place a rack in the upper third of the oven. Reheat potatoes until they are piping hot, about 30 minutes. During the last 5 minutes of cooking, turn up oven to broil, and broil potatoes until lightly browned. Serve at once.

Serves: 4 to 6 people as a side dish.

Stir-Fried Garden Vegetables

LONG-COOKING VEGETABLES
Asparagus (thick stalks), broccoli, Brussels sprouts, carrots, cauliflower, eggplant (see Note), green beans

SHORT-COOKING VEGETABLES
Asparagus (thin stalks), cabbage (bok choy, celery cabbage, green and red head cabbage), celery, Chinese long beans, corn kernels, mushrooms (button, enoki, oyster, shiitake), onions (green onions, yellow onions, red onions), peas (shelled sweet peas, snow peas, sugar-snap peas), peppers (all types of sweet peppers and chiles), squash (pattypan, yellow summer squash, zucchini), fresh water chestnuts

Stir-fried vegetables—brilliantly colored, crisp, and glistening with a sauce—are one of the healthiest, easiest vegetable side dishes to accompany any American or Asian entrée. Keep the vegetable stir-fry simple by limiting yourself to no more than three vegetables. Cut the vegetables to the same shape and size so they cook evenly. Stir-fry no more than five cups of vegetables at the same time, or they will turn to mush as they begin to boil in their own juices. Thus, if you want to serve a stir-fried vegetable dish to eight people, double the amount, and, aided by a friend, cook the vegetables in two woks simultaneously.

Follow the outline, which lists vegetables commonly found in our supermarkets, or experiment with the growing number of Asian vegetables available. To vary the flavor of this dish, replace the stir-fry sauce given here with any of the stir-fry sauces used in Chapter 5.

PREPARATION

Cut one or more types of vegetable to the same shape and size, not to exceed a total of 5 cups. The smaller the vegetables are cut, the quicker they will cook and the better the dish will look.

If choosing long-cooking vegetables, bring 2 quarts of water to a rapid boil. Cut and drop one type of vegetable at a time into the water. As soon as the vegetables brightens in color (1 to 2 minutes), immediately transfer to ice water. Repeat process with other types of long-cooking vegetables. Pat dry, then combine with any short-cooking vegetables you have chosen.

Set aside any fragile vegetables. Combine the sauce ingredients in a small bowl. *Can be completed to this point up to 8 hours in advance of Last-Minute Cooking.*

FRAGILE VEGETABLES
Bean sprouts, torn leafy greens
   (lettuce, spinach)

SAUCE
(or choose a sauce from one of
   your favorite stir-fry dishes)
1/4 cup Chinese rice wine or
   dry sherry
2 tablespoons oyster sauce
1 tablespoon dark sesame oil
1/2 teaspoon sugar
1/4 teaspoon freshly ground
   black pepper

TO FINISH
1 tablespoon cornstarch
2 tablespoons flavorless
   cooking oil
Few cloves garlic and/or 1
   tablespoon finely minced
   ginger

LAST-MINUTE COOKING

Combine the cornstarch with an equal amount of cold water and set aside. Place a wok over highest heat. When the wok is very hot, add the cooking oil to the center, then add the garlic and/or ginger. Sauté for a few seconds, then add the blanched long-cooking and the short-cooking vegetables. Stir-fry until short-cooking vegetables brighten, about 2 minutes.

Pour in the sauce. When it comes to a low boil, stir in a little of the cornstarch mixture, so that the sauce lightly glazes the vegetables. Stir in any fragile vegetables. Taste and adjust the seasonings, then spoon onto a heated platter or individual plates. Serve at once.

NOTE: Eggplant is an exception, for it should be neither blanched nor stir-fried in an open wok. Set aside 3 to 5 cups eggplant cut into 1/4-inch-thick pieces about 1 inch long. When the oil in the wok is hot, first stir-fry the eggplant (and plenty of minced garlic) for 2 minutes, then add the sauce and a splash of Chinese rice wine, dry sherry, broth, or water. Cover and cook over highest heat until the eggplant softens (about 5 minutes), adding more liquid if necessary to prevent scorching. If you want, add just a few blanched long-cooking vegetables and/or a few short-cooking vegetables. Stir-fry for about 1 minutes to heat, then tip onto platter or plates and serve.

Serves: 4 as a vegetable dish with any meat or seafood entrée.

Spicy Noodles with Asian Wraps

8 ounces dried angel-hair pasta
3 tablespoons flavorless
   cooking oil
4 ounces fresh shiitake
   mushrooms
2 medium carrots
1 cup shredded green cabbage
   (about ¼ cabbage)
¼ pound ground lamb or pork
3 cloves garlic, finely minced
2 teaspoons finely minced ginger

SAUCE
⅓ cup chicken broth, preferably
   homemade (see page 69)
¼ cup Chinese rice wine or dry
   sherry
1 tablespoon light soy sauce
1 tablespoon Asian chile sauce
2 teaspoons dark soy sauce
2 teaspoons dark sesame oil
2 teaspoons cornstarch
¼ teaspoon sugar
½ cup finely minced green
   onions, white and green
   parts
¼ cup minced cilantro sprigs

TO FINISH
8 Peking Chive Pancakes
   (page 150) or flour tortillas
½ cup hoisin sauce

Noodle stir-frys make great work-night dinners. Just boil, drain, and chill the noodles by rinsing with cold water. After the noodles are thoroughly drained, toss with any mixture of short-cooking vegetables such as pencil-thin asparagus, shredded cabbage, matchstick-cut summer squash, colorful bell peppers, or thinly sliced firm mushrooms. To cook, stir-fry in a hot wok until the vegetables brighten, add one of the stir-fry sauces from this book, and continue tossing and stirring until the noodles are thoroughly heated. While in this recipe, the noodles are wrapped in Peking Chive Pancakes, flour tortillas also work well; the noodle dish is also excellent served without any wraps.

ADVANCE PREPARATION

Bring 4 quarts of water to a rapid boil and drop in noodles. Cook until they lose their raw taste but are still firm, about 3 minutes. Drain, rinse with cold water, and drain again. Toss the noodles with 1 tablespoon of the cooking oil.

   Discard the mushroom stems; cut caps into ¼-inch strips. Cut the carrots on a sharp diagonal into very thin slices; overlap the slices and shred the carrot. Shred the cabbage. Combine the noodles with the vegetables in a large bowl, toss to combine, and refrigerate. Combine the lamb with the garlic and ginger, mixing thoroughly; refrigerate. Combine the sauce ingredients in a small bowl, mix well, and refrigerate. Wrap the pancakes or tortillas in aluminum foil so they are airtight, and refrigerate. *Can be completed to this point up to 8 hours in advance of Last-Minute Cooking.*

LAST-MINUTE COOKING

Heat oven to 325°. Heat the pancakes or tortillas in the oven for 8 to 12 minutes.

   Place a wok over highest heat. Add the remaining 2 tablespoons of oil. As it begins to heat, add the lamb and stir-fry, pressing the meat against the sides of the wok, until it loses its raw color and separates into small pieces, about 3 minutes. Add the noodle mixture and stir-fry until the noodles and meat are evenly combined, about 2 minutes. Pour in the sauce. Bring to a low boil. Taste and adjust the seasonings. Turn out onto a heated platter or individual plates. Spread each pancake or tortilla with 1 tablespoon hoisin sauce, then add 1 cup of the noodles and roll into a cylinder. Serve at once.

Serves: 4 as a pasta dish with any meat or seafood entrée.

Spicy Noodles with Asian Wraps

Asian Noodle Magic

8 ounces dried spaghetti-style
    noodles
2 tablespoons flavorless
    cooking oil
2 cups short-cooking vegetables
    (see Stir-Fried Garden
    Vegetables, page 134)
3 cloves garlic, minced
1 small shallot, minced
1 cup fresh basil leaves
2 tablespoons white sesame
    seeds
1 tablespoon cornstarch

SAUCE
3 tablespoons Chinese rice wine
    or dry sherry
3 tablespoons tomato sauce
2 tablespoons light soy sauce
2 tablespoons fresh lime juice
2 tablespoons dark brown sugar
1 teaspoon lime zest, grated or
    finely minced
1/2 teaspoon Asian chile sauce
Salt to taste

Late one afternoon, we raced along the Chao Phya River in a long, narrow "speedy boat" propelled by a giant outboard engine. Just past the Temple of Dawn, the turmoil of Bangkok slipped away as the boat disappeared into a maze of narrow canals. The pink light of the setting sun cast an ethereal color on orchid farms, tropical palm forests, teakwood houses on stilts, children swimming among the water hyacinths, and ancient ladies propelling vegetable-laden boats. Interrupting our return to the hotel, we stopped at a waterfront restaurant to snack on stir-fried noodles with basil, chile, and lime. This simple recipe, with its distinct flavors, is a good pasta dish to serve alongside either an American or Asian entrée.

ADVANCE PREPARATION

Bring 4 quarts of water to a vigorous boil. Lightly salt the water and add the noodles. Cook the noodles until they lose their raw taste but are still firm, about 5 minutes. Immediately drain in a colander, rinse with cold water, and drain again. Toss the noodles with 1 tablespoon of the cooking oil. Choose one or more short-cooking vegetables and cut into enough slivers to fill 2 cups. In a large bowl, toss the noodles with the vegetables until evenly combined, then refrigerate.

In a bowl, combine the garlic and shallot. Set aside the basil in the refrigerator. Over high heat, sauté the sesame seeds in a small skillet until they turn golden; immediately transfer to a container and set aside. Set aside the cornstarch. In a small bowl, combine sauce ingredients and refrigerate. *Can be completed to this point up to 8 hours in advance of Last-Minute Cooking.*

LAST-MINUTE COOKING

Sliver the basil leaves. Mix the cornstarch with an equal amount of cold water. Place a 12-inch sauté pan or wok over high heat. Add the remaining 1 tablespoon oil, and the garlic and shallots and sauté for 15 seconds; when the garlic begins to sizzle, add the noodle mixture. Sauté until the vegetables brighten, about 1 minute.

Stir in the basil, sesame seeds, and sauce. Stir and toss until very hot. Add a little of the cornstarch solution and cook until the noodles are glazed with the sauce. Taste and adjust the seasonings, especially for salt, then serve at once.

Serves: 2 as a pasta dish with any meat or seafood entrée.

Jade Noodles

½ pound dried spaghetti-style
   noodles
2 tablespoons flavorless
   cooking oil
1 red bell pepper

SAUCE
1½ cup packed spinach leaves,
   stemmed, washed and dried
2 cloves garlic, minced
¼ cup cilantro sprigs
10 fresh basil leaves
1 small green onion, white and
   green parts
½ cup heavy cream or chicken
   broth, preferably homemade
   (page 69)
2 tablespoons Chinese rice wine
   or dry sherry
2 tablespoons white vinegar
2 tablespoons dark sesame oil
1 tablespoon light soy sauce
2 teaspoons sugar
½ teaspoon Asian chile sauce

The brilliant green of this Asian variation on pesto sauce makes for a pasta dish that can be the visual centerpiece of a meal. The green color is most intense when a blender rather than a food processor is used. This easy, robust noodle dish is a great accompaniment to grilled fish or barbecued meat. A Pacific Flavors menu welcoming home world travelers might be Asian Roasted Red Pepper Salad, Barbecued Veal Chops with Macadamia Nuts accompanied by Jade Noodles, and, for dessert, Lemon Ice Cream.

ADVANCE PREPARATION

Bring 4 quarts of water to a rapid boil and drop in noodles. Cook until they lose their raw taste but are still firm, about 5 minutes. Drain, rinse with cold water, and drain again. Toss the noodles with 1 tablespoon of the cooking oil.

Stem, seed, and chop the red pepper; set aside. Place all the sauce ingredients in an electric blender and blend at highest speed until liquefied. If the sauce is not bright green, add more spinach leaves and blend again. Transfer to a bowl and refrigerate. *Can be completed to this point up to 8 hours in advance of Last-Minute Cooking.*

LAST-MINUTE COOKING

Place a sauté pan or wok over highest heat. Add the remaining 1 tablespoon cooking oil. When very hot, add the noodle mixture. Sauté for about 3 minutes, until the noodles begin to heat.

Add the sauce. Stir and mix until evenly combined and the noodles are very hot. Taste and adjust the seasonings. Transfer to a heated platter or individual plates. Sprinkle with chopped red pepper. Serve at once.

Serves: 4 as a pasta dish with any meat or seafood entrée.

Pacific-Style Tamales

12 dried corn husks
1 tablespoon finely minced
   ginger
½ pound fillet of Chilean sea
   bass, sole, or salmon,
   skinned
1 large egg white
¾ teaspoon salt
⅛ teaspoon Asian chile sauce
1½ cups heavy cream, very cold
2 ears white corn, husked
Tropical Fruit Salsa (page 39)

At the Authentic Cafe, Los Angeles's version of the space bar from Star Wars, *businessmen in three-piece suits reading the* Wall Street Journal, *young couples in dreadlocks, and stars from television soap operas sit elbow to elbow eating everything from tamales to spicy Chinese dumplings. This recipe was inspired by one of chef-owner Roger Hayot's creations. The seafood mousse, studded with fresh corn kernels, lies hidden inside the corn husks. This is a great side dish to serve with one of the soups from Chapter 3 and a big garden salad.*

ADVANCE PREPARATION

Soak the corn husks in cold water for 1 hour, then pat dry. Cut the fish into 1-inch cubes and place in a food processor. Add the ginger, egg white, salt, and chile sauce; puree the mixture, then place the processor bowl in the refrigerator for 2 hours or in the freezer for 30 minutes. Return the processor bowl to the machine, turn the machine on, and slowly pour the chilled cream down the feed tube in a thin stream. Scrape the sides of the processor bowl and blend again until the mixture is homogeneous.

    Stand the ears of corn on one end and cut off the kernels. You should have approximately 1 cup. Stir the kernels into the mousse. Open a corn husk flat on a work surface. Place approximately ¼ to ⅓ cup mousse in the center of the husk and fold the edges inward. Fold the husk over to close. (The mousse will expand a little during steaming, so do not over-fill the husk.) Tie the husk closed with string or thinly sliced corn husk. Fold the remaining tamales and refrigerate. Prepare the salsa. *Can be completed to this point up to 8 hours in advance of Last-Minute Cooking.*

LAST-MINUTE COOKING

Bring 3 quarts of water to a low boil in a Chinese steamer. Place the tamales on the steamer tier, place the tier over boiling water, cover, and cook about 12 minutes over high heat. Serve the tamales with Tropical Fruit Salsa.

Serves: 8 as an appetizer or 4 as a side dish with salad and soup.

*Pacific-Style Tamales with New Age Guacamole
and Tropical Fruit Salsa*

Asian Mushroom Pasta

8 ounces dried rotelle or penne
1 tablespoon flavorless
    cooking oil
6 tablespoons (³/₄ stick)
    unsalted butter
1 pound small fresh button
    mushrooms
¹/₂ pound portobello mushrooms
¹/₄ pound fresh shiitake
    mushrooms
1 bunch chives, chopped
4 cloves garlic, minced
¹/₄ cup minced shallots

SAUCE
¹/₂ cup chicken broth, preferably
    homemade (page 69) or heavy
    cream
¹/₂ cup Chinese rice wine or dry
    sherry
2 tablespoons green
    peppercorns, rinsed of brine
    and drained (optional)
1 tablespoon oyster sauce
1 tablespoon dark sesame oil
2 teaspoons cornstarch
1 teaspoon tomato paste
¹/₂ teaspoon sugar
¹/₄ teaspoon freshly ground
    black pepper
Salt to taste

Napa: Fields of mustard growing among the grapevines, pine-covered hills rising from the valley floor, old stone wineries, great homes at the end of long drives lined with liquidambar trees, hot-air balloons silhouetted against the blue sky on early winter mornings, great restaurants, and spirited wine auctions—nowhere else in America is there such passion for making fine wines and matching them with great food. This is a winter dish I particularly look forward to preparing after an adventure hunting for mushrooms with our local mushroom expert in the hills behind our home in Napa. A mixture of store-bought mushrooms creates equally good results.

ADVANCE PREPARATION

Bring at least 4 quarts of water to a vigorous boil. Lightly salt the water and add the noodles. Cook until they lose their raw taste but are still firm, about 8 minutes. Immediately drain in a colander and rinse with cold water. Drain again and stir in the cooking oil; transfer to a bowl and refrigerate. Discard the stems from the portobello and shiitake mushrooms; cut all the mushrooms into ¹/₄-inch slices and refrigerate together. Set aside the chives. Combine the garlic and shallots. Combine all of the sauce ingredients except salt in a small bowl, and refrigerate. *Can be completed to this point up to 8 hours in advance of Last-Minute Cooking.*

LAST-MINUTE COOKING

Place a 12-inch sauté pan over high heat. Add the butter, garlic, and shallots. When the garlic sizzles, about 15 seconds, add the mushrooms and sauté until they soften, about 8 minutes. Add the sauce and bring to a vigorous boil.

Transfer the pasta to the sauté pan. Stir and toss until the pasta is thoroughly reheated. Taste and adjust seasonings, particularly for salt. Transfer to a heated platter or dinner plates, sprinkle with chives, and serve at once.

MENU IDEAS: Wild Mushroom Pasta is a wonderful dish served with barbecued or roasted meats, with broiled fish, or as a vegetarian dinner accompanied by a big garden salad.

Serves: 2 as a pasta dish with any meat or seafood entrée.

Champagne Rice Pilaf

1½ cups long-grain white rice
   (not instant or converted)
4 cloves garlic, finely minced
¼ cup minced shallots
3 tablespoons unsalted butter
1 cup dried currants
1 red bell pepper, seeded and
   chopped
½ cup minced green onions,
   white and green parts
¼ cup chopped fresh basil
   leaves
¼ cup white sesame seeds

SAUCE
1 cup chicken broth, preferably
   homemade (page 69)
1½ cups good-quality
   Champagne
2 tablespoons light soy sauce
1 teaspoon freshly grated
   nutmeg
½ teaspoons Asian chile sauce
½ teaspoon salt
¼ teaspoon ground cloves

Rice cooked "pilaf style" means sautéing a long-grain white rice in butter or oil, which keeps every grain separate, and then simmering it in a seasoned broth until the liquid is entirely absorbed. This recipe uses Champagne, which contributes a wonderful yeasty taste, but the rice is also excellent when made with chicken broth or water in which dried mushrooms have soaked. However, don't ruin the recipe by using instant rice. Make a statement for good taste and purchase a premium long-grain white rice such as Thai jasmine rice, Indian basmati rice, or long-grain rice from California or Texas.

ADVANCE PREPARATION

Place the rice in a sieve. Rinse under cold water, stirring with your fingers until the water is no longer cloudy, about 2 minutes. Drain thoroughly. Set aside the garlic and shallots with the butter. Set aside the currants. Combine the red pepper, green onion, and basil in a bowl, then refrigerate. Place the sesame seeds in a small sauté pan, set over high heat, and sauté until golden. Immediately tip out and set aside. Combine the sauce ingredients in a small bowl and refrigerate. *Can be completed to this point up to 8 hours in advance of Last-Minute Cooking.*

LAST-MINUTE COOKING

Place a 3-quart saucepan over medium-high heat. Add the garlic, shallots, and butter and sauté until the butter sizzles. Add the rice and stir until coated with butter and heated through, about 5 minutes. Add the currants and sauce mixture. Bring to a low boil, stirring. Cover, reduce the heat to the lowest setting, and simmer until all the liquid is absorbed, 18 to 25 minutes. Remove the cover. Stir in the pepper, green onions, basil, and sesame seeds. Serve at once.

Serves: 6 as a rice dish for any meat or seafood entrée.

Really Risque Rice

4 cups cold cooked rice
  (about 1 cup raw)
1 cup dried currants
12 small button mushrooms
1 red bell pepper, seed, and
  diced
3 green onions, white and green
  parts, minced
½ cup pine nuts
3 large eggs, beaten
4 tablespoons flavorless
  cooking oil

SAUCE
3 tablespoons tomato sauce
2 tablespoons Chinese rice wine
  or dry sherry
1 tablespoon oyster sauce
1 tablespoon dark sesame oil
½ teaspoon sugar
½ teaspoon Asian chile sauce
  (optional)

To avoid a mushy-tasting fried rice, it's important to use thoroughly chilled cooked rice. Plan ahead. Cook the rice according to the instructions on the package, then refrigerate it for at least 4 hours. Once the rice has been chilled, make this recipe or create your own fried-rice statement. Add 2 cups of asparagus that have been cut into pieces on a sharp diagonal and then blanched in boiling water and chilled. Sauté ½ pound of raw shrimp until they turn pink, set them aside, and return the shrimp to the wok during the final minutes of stir-frying the rice. Or stir ½ pound of fresh lump crabmeat into the rice at the very end of the cooking.

ADVANCE PREPARATION

Place the cooked rice in a plastic food bag and then squeeze the bag to break the rice into little pieces; refrigerate. Set aside the currants. Thinly slice the mushrooms. Combine the mushrooms, pepper, and green onion in a bowl, then refrigerate. Toast the pine nuts until golden in a 325°F oven for about 8 minutes. Beat the eggs and refrigerate. Set aside the cooking oil. Combine the sauce ingredients, mix well, and refrigerate. *Can be completed to this point up to 8 hours in advance of Last-Minute Cooking.*

LAST-MINUTE COOKING

Place a wok over highest heat. When the wok is very hot, add 1 table-spoon of the oil to the center. Tilt the wok to coat the sides and then add eggs. Scramble the eggs, and when well scrambled, transfer to a plate.

Return the wok to highest heat and add the remaining 3 tablespoons oil. Add the vegetables and stir-fry until the pepper turns a brighter color, about 1 minute. Add the rice and currants. Stir-fry the rice and mix it evenly with the vegetables, about 1 minute.

Add the sauce. Stir-fry for 30 seconds, then add the eggs and the pine nuts. Break the eggs into smaller pieces with the edge of the spoon and continue stir-frying until everything is evenly combined and well heated. Spoon onto a heated platter or individual plates. Serve at once.

MENU IDEAS: Really Risqué Rice is excellent served with barbecued chicken, corn on the cob, and an American-style salad.

Serves: 4 as a side dish to any meat or seafood entrée.

Really Risqué Rice

Wild Rice, Pacific Style

1 cup pecan halves

SAUCE
3½ cups chicken broth,
  preferably homemade
  (see page 69)
¼ cup Chinese rice wine or
  dry sherry
2 tablespoons light soy sauce
½ teaspoon Asian chile sauce
½ teaspoon salt
1 teaspoon grated or finely
  minced orange zest

½ cup cilantro sprigs or fresh
  basil leaves
3 tablespoons unsalted butter
3 cloves garlic, finely minced
1½ cups wild rice
⅔ cup dried currants
½ cup minced green onion,
  white and green parts

This is a beautiful rice dish alive with the flavors of garlic, pecans, cilantro, chile, and grated orange zest. Some gourmet shops sell a blend of brown rice, red rice, and wild rice that works wonderfully in this recipe. But since different types of rice vary in cooking time, use just one type unless you can find the packaged multigrain mix. In this recipe, we use wild rice. But whatever rice or rice blend you use, check it during cooking, and if the liquid is gone before the rice is tender, add a little more chicken broth or water.

ADVANCE PREPARATION

Heat the oven to 325° and toast the pecans for 15 minutes, then set aside. In a small bowl, combine the sauce ingredients and mix well. *Can be completed to this point up to 8 hours in advance of Last-Minute Cooking.*

LAST-MINUTE COOKING

Chop the cilantro. Melt the butter in a 2½-quart saucepan over medium-high heat. Add the garlic and sauté for a few seconds. Add the rice and cook, stirring, until heated through, about 5 minutes. Add the currants and sauce. Bring to a low boil, stirring occasionally. Cover, reduce the heat to low, and simmer until the rice is tender, about 45 minutes. Add a few tablespoons of water or broth toward the end of the cooking if rice seems about to scorch. Stir in the cilantro, green onions, and pecans. Serve at once. (Or, refrigerate the rice until ready to serve and reheat in the microwave.)

MENU IDEAS: Serve this with one of the barbecued salmon recipes from Chapter 4, a simple salad of mixed greens, and, for dessert, fresh berries with chocolate candies.

Serves: 6 as a side dish or any meat or seafood entrée.

New Wave Garlic Bread

8 tablespoons (1 stick) unsalted
   butter
1 teaspoon Asian chile sauce
1/2 teaspoon ground Sichuan
   pepper
8 cloves garlic, finely minced
1 bunch chives, minced
1/3 cup minced cilantro sprigs
French bread, 1-foot loaf
1/2 cup grated imported
   Parmesan

If you are looking for a great garlic-bread recipe, try this one. Using fresh garlic, herbs, and the best-quality Parmesan helps create a treat that will have hungry teenagers lining up at your front door. A really easy menu with almost everything done on the barbecue would be: Smoked Rib-Eye Steaks with Ginger-Mango Salsa, New Wave Garlic Bread, a green salad tossed with an oil-and-vinegar dressing, and vanilla-bean ice cream. As a variation, use this herb-butter mix to brush across fish, shrimp, or portobello mushrooms cooking on the barbecue.

PREPARATION AND COOKING

In a small saucepan over low heat, place the butter, chile sauce, Sichuan pepper, and garlic. Heat the butter until it bubbles around the edges of the pan. Remove from the heat and stir in the chives and cilantro.

Split the bread in half lengthwise. Brush on a thin layer of the butter sauce. Add a generous amount of cheese to one half. Shake the bread to evenly coat with the cheese. Repeat with the second half.

Toast the bread on a barbecue or under the broiler until golden. Cut into slices and serve.

Serves: 8 as a side dish.

OVERLEAF: *Ingredients for Wild Rice, Pacific Style*

Peking Chive Pancakes

4 cups unbleached all-purpose
  flour
3 tablespoons finely minced
  chives
2 teaspoons crushed dried
  red-pepper flakes (optional)
1¾ cup boiling water
½ cup dark sesame oil

Peking pancakes are northern China's equivalent of the flour tortilla. But what fun it is to add minced chives, dried chile flakes, or orange zest so the plain surface is spotted with color accents and flavor surprises. When one side is rubbed with a little hoisin sauce or another condiment, Peking Chive Pancakes work wonderfully as a wrapping for stir-fry dishes, barbecued meats, and Asian salads. As a substitute use flour tortillas or mu shu wrappers, which are available frozen at most Asian markets.

The secret to making these pancakes without difficulty lies, first, in rolling out the dough into a thin sheet and cutting out circles with a wineglass. This makes every pancake an identical size. Second, if you roll the cut circles on an oiled rather than floured surface, the pancakes can be enlarged effortlessly. Use a rolling pin with handles so the rolling process goes quickly. Since there is no deterioration in the quality of the pancakes after repeated freezing and thawing, store extra batches in the freezer for spontaneous meals.

ADVANCE PREPARATION

Place the flour, chives, and dried red-pepper flakes, if using, in a bowl. Add all the boiling water and stir briefly. Turn the dough out onto a lightly floured board or smooth countertop and knead until smooth and elastic. Cover for 15 minutes.

Roll out the dough on a lightly floured surface to ¼ inch, occasionally turning the dough over. Then, with a 3-inch wineglass or round cookie cutter, cut the dough into 30 disks.

Thoroughly clean the work surface and lightly rub with ½ tablespoon sesame oil. Place a disk on the oiled counter and rub about ½ teaspoon sesame oil over it. Lay another disk on top. Using your palm, gently press the 2 disks together. Roll the pair into an 8-inch round. Always roll from the center of the disk out to the edge, changing direction after each rolling motion, in order to stretch the dough into a large disk. Do not turn the dough during this process.

Heat a 12-inch skillet over medium heat. Add the double pancake and cook for about 45 seconds on one side. Flip the pancake over and cook for about 15 seconds on the other side. The pancake is done when it loses its raw color; it should have only a few brown spots (if there are lots of brown spots, this is a sign of too-high heat or too long a cooking time).

Remove the double pancake from the pan and, starting on one edge, gently pull the 2 layers apart. Stack them directly on top of each other (they will not stick together) and cover with a towel. Repeat the rolling and cooking process with the rest of the dough. Wrap the stack of Peking Chive Pancakes in plastic wrap or foil. Refrigerate for up to 5 days or freeze indefinitely.

California Cornbread

1½ cups yellow cornmeal
½ cup all-purpose flour
2 teaspoons baking powder
1 teaspoon salt
3 large eggs, well beaten
1¼ cups milk
5½ tablespoons unsalted butter, melted
¼ cup honey
½ cup dried currants
3 cloves garlic, finely minced
1 teaspoon grated or minced tangerine or orange zest
Kernels from 1 ear of corn
¼ cup minced cilantro sprigs

On our first trip outside of California, we were shocked to discover that what most Americans call cornbread has no garlic, no beautiful flecks of tangerine zest, no crunchy sweet kernels of corn, no green specks of cilantro, and no currants! What has happened to good cooking? What an outrage that a great recipe has been so simplified it is currently fit only for hospitals or the convalescent homes. Here in California, the original cornbread, nurtured by generations of our cooks, warms our tummies. Serve California Cornbread with plenty of honey butter and accompany it with barbecued meat or a dish with lots of sauce.

PREPARATION AND COOKING

Heat the oven to 400°F. In a large mixing bowl, thoroughly combine the cornmeal, flour, baking powder, and salt. In a separate bowl, combine the beaten eggs, milk, melted butter, and honey. Mix well, then add the remaining ingredients and mix again. Stir liquid ingredients into the cornmeal mixture and mix just until dry ingredients are moistened, leaving plenty of lumps.

Butter a 10-inch-diameter iron skillet and heat for 15 minutes in the oven. (Using a heavy skillet and heating it gives the cornbread a crunchy exterior.) When heated, pour in the batter. Bake for about 30 minutes. The cornbread is done when a knife pushed deep into the center comes out clean. Cut into slices and serve with butter and honey.

Serves: 6 as a side dish to any meat or seafood entrée.

Magic Mousse and Chocolate Chip Macadamia Nut Cookies

Sinful Sweets

God created desserts and, as an afterthought, added the preliminary dishes. But not all desserts were created equal, for it is said that on the long dessert tables crisscrossing the Garden of Eden, chocolate was king. In the time of darkness and turmoil that followed the apple affair, no longer did days commence with chocolate, continue with chocolate, and conclude with chocolate. Charlatans spread myths about calories, preached the evils of fat, and established diet centers. Guilt was everywhere.

Now a great period of enlightenment comes upon us, foretelling of Judgment Day when once again a person's wealth will be determined by the amount of chocolate stored in the chocolate cellar. Fathers will thrust little chunks of chocolate into the upraised hands of their newborn. Our lives will be enriched by chocolate lotteries, chocolate holidays, and chocolate currency. Anticipate this glorious age with these luscious homemade ice creams, buttery chocolate-chip cookies, and extra-rich chocolate desserts. Serve these sweets anytime, and sin again.

Magic Mousse

¼ cup finely freshly ground
   coffee beans
½ cup boiling water
2 ounces bittersweet chocolate,
   cut into small pieces
4 large eggs, separated
½ cup sugar
¼ cup Grand Marnier
1 tablespoon unflavored gelatin
1 cup heavy cream
Raspberry Cabernet Sauvignon
   Sauce (page 160),
   thoroughly chilled
Fresh raspberries, chocolate
   shavings, and whipped
   cream, for garnish

The chocolate mousse in Julia Child's Mastering the Art of French Cooking, *with its flavors of rich chocolate, Grand Marnier, and espresso, has a lingering ethereal taste. The same flavor combination is used to make this very easy mousse. Layers of mousse, piped through a pastry tube into wineglasses, alternate with Raspberry Cabernet Sauvignon Sauce. When the mousse is garnished with fresh raspberries, whipped cream, and chocolate shavings, your friends will murmur "magical . . . magical!"*

ADVANCE PREPARATION

Place the ground coffee in a cup, add boiling water, stir, cover, and steep for 10 minutes. Place ¼ cup of the coffee, 2 teaspoons of the coffee grounds, and the chocolate in a small, heatproof bowl (discard remaining coffee and grounds). Melt over simmering water, stir until thoroughly blended, and then keep warm over hot water; or melt in a microwave-safe bowl in the microwave oven at low power.

In a stainless-steel or copper mixing bowl, vigorously beat the egg yolks and sugar until the mixture turns pale yellow, about 3 minutes. Beat in the Grand Marnier and gelatin. Place the mixing bowl over a saucepan of simmering water and stir the mixture until it becomes hot to the touch, about 4 minutes. Remove from the simmering water and stir in the chocolate mixture.

Beat the egg whites until stiff peaks form. Stir one-fourth of the egg whites into the chocolate mixture, then gently fold in the remaining whites one-third at a time. Beat the cream until stiff, and then gently fold into the mousse.

Transfer the mousse to a pastry bag fitted with a large tube. Pipe a little of the mousse into the bottom of eight wineglasses. Add a very thin layer of Cabernet Sauvignon Raspberry Sauce, then a thick layer of mousse, a thin layer of sauce, and finish with another thick layer of mousse. Refrigerate for at least 3 hours. *Can be completed to this point up to 8 hours in advance of serving.*

SERVING

Garnish the top of each mousse with one or any combination of the following: chocolate shavings, fresh raspberries, or stiffly beaten whipped cream piped through a pastry tube.

Serves: 8.

Chocolate Chip Macadamia Nut Cookies

4 ounces roasted macadamia nuts

8 tablespoons (1 stick) unsalted butter, softened

½ cup light brown sugar

¼ cup granulated sugar

1 large egg

1 teaspoon pure vanilla extract

¾ teaspoon baking powder

½ teaspoon baking soda

½ teaspoon salt

½ cup chopped crystallized ginger

8 ounces white or dark chocolate chips or chunks

1½ cups all-purpose flour

What happier childhood memories remain than those of scooping chocolate-chip-cookie batter from the mixing bowl, or surreptitiously seizing hot cookies from the baking sheet, or lazing on your bed in the heat of a summer afternoon, conducting a quality-control test on mounds of cookies? Re-create childhood and whip up a batch of these cookies, filled with chocolate, macadamia nuts, and crystallized ginger. As a variation, form the batter into one giant cookie and bake for 30 minutes. Served on a huge plate, this mega-cookie always evokes laughs from dinner guests as they break off sections.

PREPARATION

If the nuts are salted, rinse briefly and pat dry; chop. Combine the butter and sugars in a large bowl; stir until thoroughly blended. Add the egg, vanilla, baking powder, baking soda, and salt. Stir well. Add the crystallized ginger, chocolate chips, and nuts, then stir again. Add the flour one-third at a time and mix thoroughly. *Can be completed to this point for up to a week if refrigerated or indefinitely if frozen.*

BAKING

Heat oven to 350°F. Butter a baking sheet or line it with parchment paper. Scoop out the cookie dough 2 tablespoons at a time, and place an inch apart on the baking sheet. Bake until light golden, about 12 minutes. Let cool on a rack. They can be served later, if you can wait, or eaten at once.

Makes: 24 cookies.

Mango Ice Cream

6 large egg yolks
1 cup sugar
3 cups heavy cream
4 ripe mangos
2 teaspoons pure vanilla extract

To Serve
Chocolate Grand Marnier Sauce
   (optional, page 159)
Mint sprigs

High above the outdoor barbecue at the Oriental Hotel, bursts of fireworks illuminate Bangkok's skyline, while along the Chao Phya River thousands of lotus-shaped "boats," each containing a lighted candle, incense, and flowers, bob in swirling patterns. As the Thai celebrate the most enchanting of all their festivals and give thanks to the Mother of Water, a few feet away our band of Americans, pilgrims abroad, join together for Thanksgiving. Long after we have consumed platters of barbecued lobster, pad Thai noodle salad seasoned with lime, crisp banana fritters, and mango ice cream, we watch the festival of lights.

ADVANCE PREPARATION

Make the ice cream: In a copper or stainless-steel mixing bowl, vigorously whisk the egg yolks and sugar until the mixture turns a pale yellow, about 3 minutes. Fill a large bowl or sink with cold water and add a generous amount of ice. Heat the cream in a 3-quart saucepan until bubbles appear around the edges. Slowly whisk into the egg mixture. Briefly beat the mixture and pour it back into the saucepan. Place the empty mixing bowl in the ice water.

Place the saucepan over high heat and whisk the mixture quickly until it becomes thick enough to lightly coat a spoon and nearly doubles in volume, about 4 minutes. (Be sure to stir vigorously, and do not overcook the custard, or the yolks will curdle.) Immediately tip the custard into the chilled mixing bowl and whisk slowly for 2 minutes. Refrigerate for at least 2 hours.

Using a paring knife, remove the mango skin. Slice off flesh, and puree in a food processor. You should have about 3 cups of puree. Set aside 1 cup of the custard; combine remaining custard with the mango puree. Stir in vanilla. Place mixture in an ice-cream maker and freeze according to manufacturer's directions. Makes 2 quarts of ice cream. Prepare the chocolate sauce, if using. *Can be completed up to 2 days in advance of assembling.*

ASSEMBLING

Place 1 large scoop or 3 small scoops of ice cream in the center of each plate. Circle with reserved custard. Drizzle some Chocolate Grand Marnier Sauce on top, if desired. Garnish with mint sprigs. Serve at once.

Serves: 8.

Mango Ice Cream and Orange Ginger Brownies
(recipe on page 158)

Orange Ginger Brownies

1 cup chopped pecans, walnuts, or macadamia nuts
$\frac{1}{2}$ pound (2 sticks) unsalted butter
4 ounces bittersweet chocolate
4 large eggs
$1\frac{1}{4}$ cups sugar
2 teaspoons pure vanilla extract
1 tablespoon grated or finely minced orange zest
4 ounces crystallized ginger candy, slivered
$\frac{1}{2}$ teaspoon salt
$\frac{1}{2}$ cup all-purpose flour
Raspberry Cabernet Sauvignon Sauce (page 160)

When we were working on a brownie recipe, someone suggested we try white chocolate. We thought, "A brownie made from white chocolate is a contradiction! Only invalids eat white chocolate!" Now, these are real *brownies, made with dark chocolate, minced orange zest, crystallized ginger, and pecans. Serve Orange Ginger Brownies with fruit or ice cream, or on dessert plates atop a glaze of Raspberry Cabernet Sauvignon Sauce.*

PREPARATION AND BAKING

Heat the oven to 350°F. Butter a 9-by-12-inch baking pan and set aside. Place the nuts on a baking sheet and toast for 10 minutes; let cool. Melt the butter, then let cool to room temperature. Cut the chocolate into small chunks, place in a small, heatproof bowl, and melt over a saucepan of simmering water, or place chocolate in a microwave-safe bowl and melt in a microwave at low power.

In a mixing bowl, combine the eggs and sugar, beating well with a whisk. Add the melted butter and chocolate, mixing again. Stir in the vanilla, orange peel, crystallized ginger, salt, and nuts. Add the flour and mix well. Pour the batter into the prepared pan. Bake in the middle of the oven until the brownies are just set in the center, about 20 to 25 minutes. Cool, cut into squares, and store in an airtight container. Prepare the sauce. *Can be completed to this point up to one day in advance of serving.*

SERVING

If brownies are the main dessert, serve with the raspberry sauce. Glaze the surface of each dessert plate with the sauce. Place a brownie in the center of each plate, then serve.

Makes: 28 brownies.

Lemon Ice Cream with Chocolate Grand Marnier Sauce

4 cups heavy cream
2 cups sugar
1 cup fresh lemon juice

**CHOCOLATE GRAND MARNIER
SAUCE**
8 ounces bittersweet chocolate
½ cup heavy cream
½ cup Grand Marnier

TO SERVE
Mint sprigs or candied lemon
    twists

Homemade ice cream is a fantastic dessert! Made with pure ingredients and without the presence of stabilizers that even the most expensive ice creams contain, it must be consumed within a few days of being churned or it will begin to crystallize. This delicious ice cream and easy recipe comes from chef Grant Showley. We like to prepare the ice cream mix ahead, and then when our dinner guests arrive, churn the ice cream with all eyes observing the action. While the inexpensive, hand-cranked Donvier (available at all cookware and department stores) works fine, we prefer the White Mountain electric ice cream machine. It's expensive, but the texture of the ice cream is unequaled. Dinner guests help sprinkle the rock salt and ice around the spinning metal cylinder, and once the ice cream is churned, lay wet beach towels over the machine so that the ice cream "cures" in its icy water bath during dinner. In this manner the evening begins with a fun informal activity, and concludes with a grand dessert that all of us have helped create.

ADVANCE PREPARATION

Beat the cream with the sugar until well mixed. Stir in the lemon juice and mix well (ignore curdled look). Place the mixture in an ice-cream maker and freeze according to the manufacturer's directions. Makes 2 quarts.

To make the sauce, cut the chocolate into small chunks. Place the chocolate and cream in a small, heatproof bowl and melt over a saucepan of simmering water. Stir until thoroughly blended, then stir in the Grand Marnier. Or place chocolate and cream in a microwave-safe bowl and melt in the microwave oven at low power. Set aside at room temperature for up to 1 hour or refrigerate. *Can be completed to this point up to one day in advance of Last-Minute Assembling.*

LAST-MINUTE ASSEMBLING

If the chocolate sauce is a little too thick to pour evenly over the dessert plates, warm over simmering water. Then glaze each dessert plate with a thin layer of the sauce. Place 1 large scoop or 3 small scoops of ice cream in the center of each plate. Garnish with mint sprigs or twists of candied lemon. Serve at once.

Serves: 12.

Raspberry Cabernet Sauvignon Tart

PASTRY DOUGH
1¼ cups all-purpose flour
½ teaspoon salt
10 tablespoons (1 stick plus 2 tablespoons) chilled unsalted butter, cut into small pieces
2–4 tablespoons ice water

4 ounces bittersweet chocolate, chopped

PASTRY CREAM
6 large egg yolks
⅔ cup sugar
1 tablespoon pure vanilla extract
2 tablespoons all-purpose flour
2 tablespoons cornstarch
2 cups milk

RASPBERRY CABERNET SAUVIGNON SAUCE
1 bottle reasonably good Cabernet Sauvignon or other red wine
12 ounces frozen raspberries
1 cup sugar
½ teaspoon freshly ground black pepper

While this is the most time-consuming recipe in the book, you can make the raspberry sauce weeks in advance and the crust a day before serving. This recipe is based on a dessert from one of California's most talented chefs, Mark Dierkhising. His Raspberry Cabernet Sauvignon Sauce is excellent on cheesecake, ice cream, pancakes, pies and tarts, and even chilled roast chicken.

ADVANCE PREPARATION

Heat the oven to 375°F. Prepare the pastry dough: Place the flour, salt, and 8 tablespoons of butter in a food processor. Process until the mixture resembles cornmeal. Add ice water a little at a time, processing only until the dough forms into little balls (don't let dough form into a large ball or it will be tough). Turn out onto plastic wrap, press into a ball, wrap, and refrigerate for 30 minutes. On a lightly floured board roll out chilled dough into a ¼-inch-thick circle. Gently fit into a 10-inch tart pan and press the dough up the sides. Remove excess dough and save for another use or discard. Cover with parchment paper and place a layer of pastry weights or beans on top. Bake for 15 minutes; remove the paper and weights and bake for about 15 minutes more, until deep golden. Remove crust from the oven and let cool to room temperature.

Place the chocolate and remaining 2 tablespoons butter in a small, heatproof bowl and melt over a saucepan of simmering water, or place in a microwave-safe bowl and melt in the microwave oven at low power. Stir until blended, then brush across the pastry shell and around the sides. Freeze until the chocolate hardens.

Prepare the pastry cream: Beat together the egg yolks and sugar until pale yellow. Beat in the vanilla, flour, and cornstarch. In a saucepan, heat the milk until bubbles appear around edges, then stir into the egg mixture. Pour back into the saucepan and place over medium-high heat. Whisk until the mixture becomes very thick, about 2 minutes. Pour into a bowl, press plastic wrap across the cream's surface, and refrigerate for at least 1 hour. Fill the tart shell with chilled pastry cream and refrigerate for at least 4 hours.

Prepare the raspberry sauce: In a 12-inch nonreactive skillet, combine all the ingredients. Bring to a vigorous boil over high heat and cook, stirring occasionally, until only 2 cups remain (about 30 minutes of rapid boiling). Using the edge of a metal spoon, force all the liquid and pulp through a medium-mesh sieve. Refrigerate for at least 3 hours. (It will last for a month refrigerated.) Makes 1⅔ cups sauce. *Can be completed up to this point up to a day in advance of assembling.*

ASSEMBLING

Warm the sauce. Pour ½ cup sauce onto the tart, and tilt the tart back and forth to glaze the top. (Can be completed to this point and refrigerated for 1 day.) Remove the sides of the tart pan. Cut the tart into wedges and serve with the remaining sauce.

Serves: 8.

Warm Chocolate Creme Brulee

4 ounces bittersweet chocolate
4 large egg yolks
⅓ cup sugar
2 cup heavy cream
1 teaspoon pure vanilla extract

TO FINISH
¼ cup sugar

There are several key steps to making perfect warm crème brûlée. The first is to cook the custard only until it sets, or the silky texture of the custard becomes curdled. Normally, when crème brûlée turns golden on top, that is a sign it's perfectly cooked. However, because this chocolate crème brûlée is already dark on the surface, you'll need to jiggle the ramekins. When the custard no longer moves, it's done. The second step is to add the sugar topping just before serving, otherwise the sugar will be absorbed by the custard and there will be nothing to caramelize. The third step is to caramelize the sugar using a blowtorch. No other technique caramelizes the sugar evenly. Small, inexpensive blowtorches are sold by all hardware stores. The final key step is to serve the crème brûlée while it is still warm; if you refrigerate it, the chocolate custard becomes too firm.

ADVANCE PREPARATION

Chop the chocolate into little pieces. In a small bowl, whisk the egg yolks with the sugar until pale yellow, about 2 minutes. Heat the cream in a small saucepan until little bubbles appear around the edges. Pour the hot cream into the eggs, stirring well. Add the chocolate and stir until completely melted. Stir in the vanilla. Pour the mixture into six ½- to ⅔-cup ovenproof ramekins. Refrigerate until ready to complete. *Can be completed to this point up to 8 hours in advance of Last-Minute Cooking.*

LAST-MINUTE COOKING

Heat the oven to 350°F. Place the ramekins in a deep baking pan and add enough hot water so that they are half submerged. Bake until the custard does not move when gently jiggled, about 40 to 50 minutes. Remove the baking pan from the oven, and remove the ramekins from the baking pan. Let rest at room temperature for at least 30 minutes but not longer than 1 hour. Just before serving, sprinkle a thin layer of sugar across the surface of each ramekin. Immediately caramelize the sugar with a blowtorch. Serve the crème brûlée at once.

Serves: 6.

Warm Polenta Cake with Zinfandel Macerated Strawberries

¹/₄ cup golden raisins
¹/₄ cup dry white wine
2 cups ricotta cheese
2 cups mascarpone cheese
1 cup sugar
1 teaspoon pure vanilla extract
1 tablespoon fennel seed, ground to a powder in a spice grinder
³/₄ cup polenta or yellow cornmeal
1 tablespoon unsalted butter
¹/₄ cup confectioners' sugar

MACERATED STRAWBERRIES
2 pints strawberries, cleaned and sliced
¹/₄ cup granulated sugar
1 cup Zinfandel or other fruity dry red wine

This dessert recipe is contributed by the talented Cakebread Winery executive chef, Brian Streeter, who has made it often with my cooking students at the winery. All the ingredients for the polenta cake are combined ahead, and then it is cooked in the oven during dinner. After being allowed to cool slightly, it is dusted with confectioners' sugar, cut into serving portions, and served warm with strawberries macerated with red wine and sugar. It is utterly delicious with a fruity red wine such as the Cakebread Zinfandel or a white dessert wine. If you do not have fresh ricotta, substitute cottage cheese, you can also substitute cream cheese for mascarpone. When substituting, use the same amounts.

ADVANCE PREPARATION

In a small saucepan, cover the raisins with white wine and bring to a boil. Immediately remove from the heat, allow to soften for 20 minutes, then drain and discard wine. In a large bowl, whisk together the cheeses, sugar, vanilla, and fennel until smooth. Stir in the polenta and raisins, and mix until evenly blended. Butter the bottom and sides of a 9-inch springform pan, pour in the batter, and refrigerate. *Can be completed to this point up to 3 hours in advance of Last-Minute Cooking.*

LAST-MINUTE COOKING

Heat the oven to 300°F. Slice the strawberries into a bowl and toss with sugar, adjusting the amount of sugar depending on the sweetness of the berries. Cover with red wine and allow to marinate at room temperature for 1 hour.

Bake the polenta cake until set, about 1 hour and 15 minutes. The cake should still be slightly liquid in the center. Remove the cake from the oven and allow to cool slightly, about 15 minutes. Dust with confectioners' sugar and cut into serving portions. Spoon the strawberries on the dessert plates, top with slices of the polenta cake, and serve at once.

Serves: 12.

Caramel Fudge Tart with Crumble Crust

6 ounces (about 8) chocolate
  graham crackers
10 tablespoons (1 stick plus 2
  tablespoons) unsalted butter
1 cup sugar
1/2 cup water
1/2 cup heavy cream

CHOCOLATE FUDGE FILLING
10 ounces bittersweet chocolate
1 cup heavy cream
2 teaspoons pure vanilla extract
2 teaspoons finely minced or
  grated orange zest
1/2 teaspoon ground cinnamon
1/4 teaspoon freshly ground
  black pepper

2 pints fresh raspberries
1 cup raspberry jam

Fresh raspberries, a rich chocolate-fudge filling, and chewy, nutty-tasting caramel sauce combine to make this divine dessert. There are many ways to utilize the parts of this recipe. The caramel sauce will last for weeks if refrigerated, and then is great warmed and poured over ice cream. Make chocolate truffles: Pour the chocolate fudge into a bowl and refrigerate. When thoroughly chilled, form the chocolate into little balls using a teaspoon, and transfer to a parchment-lined baking sheet. Sprinkle with cocoa powder while jiggling the baking sheet, so that as the balls roll across the surface, they become lightly dusted. Refrigerate and eat within 4 days.

ADVANCE PREPARATION

Heat the oven to 400°F. Melt 8 tablespoons of the butter. Crush enough graham crackers in a food processor to equal 1 1/2 cups of crumbs and transfer to a bowl. Stir in the melted butter and combine evenly. Press the crumbs into the bottom and along the sides of a 10-inch tart pan. Place the tart pan on a baking sheet, and bake for 10 minutes. Remove the pan from the oven and let cool.

Place the sugar and water in a 2-quart saucepan. Set over high heat and stir briefly. Bring to a rapid boil without stirring, and boil until the sugar turns dark brown, about 4 minutes. If the sugar begins to smoke or turn black, it will have a burned taste, and must be cooled and discarded. When the sugar turns a dark brown, remove the saucepan from the heat. Using a long-handled whisk, stir the caramel while slowly adding the cream. Stir in the remaining 2 tablespoons butter. While the caramel sauce is still hot, pour it in an even layer over the crust, and freeze for 3 hours.

Place all the ingredients for the chocolate fudge filling in a 2-quart saucepan. Set over low heat, and stir until all the chocolate has melted and the sauce is very smooth. Remove the tart shell from the freezer and pour the chocolate fudge filling over the caramel surface. Refrigerate for at least 2 hours. When the chocolate surface becomes firm, decorate the top with raspberries. Place the raspberry jam in a small saucepan and heat until it liquid; pour the sauce through a sieve to remove the seeds. Using a pastry brush, brush the raspberries with the raspberry sauce. *Can be made to this point up to one day in advance of Last-Minute Serving and refrigerated.*

LAST-MINUTE SERVING

Cut the tart into serving pieces. Serve at room temperature.

Serves: 6 to 8.

Chocolate Mudslide Cookies

³/₄ cup pecans

6 tablespoons (³/₄ stick) unsalted butter

³/₄ cup sugar

2 large eggs

4 ounces bittersweet chocolate, cut into small pieces

¹/₄ cup unsweetened cocoa powder

1 teaspoon pure vanilla extract

³/₄ teaspoon baking powder

¹/₂ teaspoon salt

¹/₄ teaspoon freshly ground black pepper

3 ounces white chocolate, cut into small pieces

³/₄ cup unbleached all-purpose flour

Oakville Grocery in Napa Valley sells dense chocolate cookies called "mudslides." Unable to wrestle the recipe from the pastry chef, we set out on a prolonged chocolate-cookie-testing binge lasting several weeks. Here is the new improved recipe! (We like to use a block of white chocolate and chop it into irregular pieces, but you could also use chips.)

ADVANCE PREPARATION

Heat the oven to 325°F. Spread the pecans on a baking sheet and toast for 15 minutes; cool to room temperature and chop. Increase the oven temperature to 350°F. Place the butter and sugar in a food processor fitted with the metal blade and process until thoroughly blended. Add the eggs and blend briefly. Place the bittersweet-chocolate pieces in a small, heatproof bowl and melt over a saucepan of simmering water, or place chocolate in a microwave-safe bowl and melt in the microwave oven on low power, stirring every 10 seconds. With the food processor on, pour the melted chocolate through the feed tube. Transfer the mixture to a bowl, and add the cocoa, vanilla, baking powder, salt, and pepper. Stir until thoroughly mixed. Stir in the nuts and white-chocolate pieces. Add the flour and stir until thoroughly mixed.

Line baking sheets with nonstick parchment paper. Using a spoon, place 2-tablespoon amounts of the dough on the paper, leaving about 2 inches between each cookie. Bake for 12 minutes, then cool on the paper. Transfer to an airtight container, cover, and store at room temperature. *Can be made one day in advance of eating.*

Makes: 2 dozen cookies.

Chocolate Decadence

8 ounces bittersweet chocolate
2 cups heavy cream
1 large egg plus 2 yolks
¼ cup Grand Marnier or
   Kahlua
4 thin slices crystallized ginger
Whipped cream or fresh
   raspberries, for garnish

This is the recipe we turn to whenever we want to minimize our dinner preparation time. It's an intensely flavored chocolate custard that is served in little chocolate pots or ramekins. Because of its richness, we eat this using demitasse spoons, and often accompany the dessert with a seasonal fruit such as raspberries.

ADVANCE PREPARATION

Place the chocolate and cream in a heavy saucepan. Heat over lowest heat, stirring slowly, until the chocolate melts. Let cool to room temperature. Whisk together the egg and yolks until thickened, about 1 minute, then stir into the chocolate mixture. Add the Grand Marnier or Kahlua.

Sliver the ginger, place a few slivers in each of eight ½-cup (4-ounce) small pots or ramekins, and add the chocolate mixture. Refrigerate for at least 2 hours. *Can be made to this point up to one day in advance of serving.*

SERVING

Decorate the tops with whipped cream or raspberries.

Serves: 6.

Cakebread Winery's Fallen Chocolate Souffle

10 ounces bittersweet chocolate
1/4 teaspoon freshly ground black pepper
1 teaspoon finely minced or grated orange zest
20 tablespoons (2½ sticks) unsalted butter, at room temperature
9 large egg yolks, room temperature
1/2 cup granulated sugar
5 large egg whites, at room temperature
1/4 teaspoon cream of tartar
Raspberry Cabernet Sauvignon Sauce (page 160)
Chocolate Grand Marnier Sauce (page 159)
1/2 cup confectioners' sugar

This soufflé is based on a recipe from Cakebread Winery's executive chef, Brian Streeter, who in turn based it on a recipe from Lindsey Shire, pastry chef at the famous Chez Panisse restaurant. Our addition is the use of black pepper, grated orange, and the raspberry and chocolate sauces. After the soufflés are removed from the oven, they are allowed to cool for a few minutes. During the cooling, the soufflés sink and their edges are pushed inwards, creating a "fallen" soufflé with a marvelous chewy texture. To bake the soufflés, Brian uses clean, empty 6-ounce pineapple cans, which are 3¼ inches in diameter, and removes their tops and bottoms. Or you could use 4-inch-diameter flan rings. After the soufflés cool slightly, they are removed from the rings and transferred to dessert plates. You could also bake the soufflés in individual buttered soufflé dishes, and serve them piping hot in the baking dishes.

ADVANCE PREPARATION

Butter a large baking sheet and butter the insides of ten 3¼- or 4-inch-diameter rings. Place the rings an inch apart on the baking sheet. Chop chocolate into small pieces and place in a small, heatproof bowl. Melt over a saucepan of simmering water, or place chocolate in a microwave-safe bowl and melt in the microwave oven on low power, stirring every 20 seconds. Stir in the pepper and grated orange zest. Place butter in a medium bowl and beat at high speed until fluffy. Beat in melted chocolate.

In a large bowl, beat egg yolks with 6 tablespoons of the sugar at high speed until the mixture is pale yellow and no sugar crystals are visible, about 5 minutes. Beat in the chocolate mixture at low speed until evenly blended.

In another large bowl, using the whisk attachment or clean beaters, beat eggs whites until foamy. Add cream of tartar and beat at medium speed until soft peaks form. Beat in remaining 2 tablespoons sugar at high speed until the whites hold soft peaks again. Using a rubber spatula, fold one-third of the whites into the chocolate mixture. Fold in remaining whites just until mixed. Fill each of the prepared rings about half full. Smooth the tops. Prepare the raspberry and chocolate sauces. *Can be made to this point up to 3 hours in advance of Last-Minute Cooking. Keep the soufflés at room temperature.*

LAST-MINUTE COOKING

In separate containers, warm the raspberry and chocolate sauces. Heat oven to 300°F. Bake soufflés until they puff and are just set in the middle, about 15 minutes for 3¼-inch rings and 20 minutes for 4-inch rings. Set baking sheet on a rack to cool. As soufflés cool, they will sink. Push in edges so that they fall evenly into the rings. After 10 minutes, remove rings from soufflés. Using a metal spatula, transfer soufflés to dessert plates. Dust tops with confectioners' sugar. Surround each soufflé with the raspberry sauce. Add a drizzle of chocolate sauce over each soufflé and serve warm.

Serves: 8.

Coconut Cream with Fresh Berries and Chocolate

1 coconut (see Note)
3 cups half-and-half
6 large egg yolks
²/₃ cup sugar
6 cups fresh berries
½ cup kirsch
Chocolate Grand Marnier
  Sauce (page 159)

Dessert plates glazed with coconut cream and mounded with fresh berries, perhaps accompanied by Chocolate Chip Macadamia Nut Cookies (page 155), would make a great finale. Now a different type of feast draws to a close. Just as the recipe for Thai Salmon Satay, which began this book, welcomed you to our love of food and entertaining, so this delicious dessert serves as our fond farewell.

ADVANCE PREPARATION AND COOKING

Puncture one of the coconut eyes and then shake out and discard the interior liquid. Place the coconut in a towel and break it against a hard surface. Using a screwdriver, pry away the flesh. With a potato peeler, remove any black surface from the flesh. Coarsely chop the flesh in a food processor. Add the half-and-half and process for 1 minute. Transfer to a saucepan and heat to just below the boiling point; then turn off the heat and set aside for 1 hour. Transfer the coconut and cream to the center of a double layer of cheesecloth placed over a 2-quart saucepan, and squeeze the cheesecloth to extract all the liquid. You will need 2 cups of coconut cream.

Fill a large bowl with cold water and ice. Place the egg yolks and sugar in a metal bowl and whisk vigorously until the mixture turns pale yellow, about 3 minutes. Place the saucepan holding the coconut cream over medium-high heat and heat until bubbles appear around the edges. Pour the liquid slowly into the egg mixture, whisking constantly. Pour the coconut-egg mixture back into the saucepan. Place the empty mixing bowl in the ice water.

Place the saucepan over high heat. Whisk quickly until the mixture becomes thick enough to lightly coat a spoon and nearly doubles in volume, about 4 minutes. (Do not overcook the custard, or the yolks will curdle.) Immediately tip the custard into the chilled mixing bowl and whisk slowly for 2 minutes. Refrigerate for at least 2 hours. *Can be completed to this point up to 24 hours in advance of Last-Minute Assembling.*

LAST-MINUTE ASSEMBLING

Toss the berries with the kirsch. Glaze eight dessert plates with the coconut cream. Warm the chocolate sauce over simmering water. Make thin lines or a circle of sauce across the surface of the coconut cream. With the tip of a skewer, cut across the lines of chocolate sauce to create swirls. Drain the berries and carefully position them in the center of each plate. Serve at once.

NOTE: Although canned coconut milk works great for most recipes, in this one the subtle flavor difference of freshly made coconut milk does produce a better-tasting dessert.

Serves: 8.

All About Woks and Stir-Frying

Wok is the Cantonese word for a practical, multipurpose, concave Chinese cooking utensil used to create a vast range of delicious dishes. Spring rolls slide down the sides into hot oil without a splash. Fish placed on an elevated rack above rapidly boiling water and covered by the domed top steams to perfection. Stews bubble gently over low heat. The sloping sides mean the wok requires less oil than Western frying pans. When given a swish, stir-fried ingredients automatically fall to the bottom, the hottest part of the wok, for quick, even cooking. Because of the pan's shape, Chinese foods, particularly stir-fried dishes, taste better than recipes made in another utensil.

Woks range from the inexpensive, traditional heavy steel type sold by Asian markets to deluxe stainless-steel and nonstick woks available at gourmet shops. If you buy a Chinese steel wok, it needs to be specially seasoned, used frequently, and carefully cleaned. After frequent use, it acquires a beautiful black luster; it is this black seasoning that makes woks nonstick and contributes a special "wok" flavor to stir-fried dishes. Or purchase a Calphalon (my favorite) stainless-steel or nonstick wok. But avoid the electric wok. Even at its highest setting, it never becomes hot enough for stir-frying, so the food just boils in its own juices.

Buy a 14- or 16-inch flat-bottomed wok with a long wooden handle on one side and a short handle on the opposite side. Without these two handles it is impossible to quickly and effortlessly tip the food out from the wok onto a serving platter. Equally important, use a flat-bottomed wok whether cooking on gas or electric stoves. The flat bottom rests securely on the stove burner, and more surface is exposed directly to the heat than if using the traditional round-bottomed wok; a flat-bottomed wok becomes much hotter, the food cooks more quickly, and the dish will taste better.

The heavy steel woks such as those made by Atlas Spinning Company, which are sold in Asian markets, require special care. These come coated with a thin layer of oil. Scrub the wok thoroughly inside and out with hot, soapy water, using a scouring pad. The wok is clean when the gray coating no longer comes off on your hands. Dry the wok, then place it over high heat. When the wok becomes hot to the touch, season it by adding a quarter cup cooking oil to the center. With a paper towel and spoon, coat the inside surface with oil; as the oil begins to smoke slightly, remove the wok from the heat. Let it cool completely, then wipe the oil from the wok. With repeated use, the wok seasoning gradually turns black, creating a nonstick surface, provided no one scrubs the seasoning off or boils water in the work for steaming, which removes the seasoning.

Clean your steel wok as you would any good omelet pan: Place it in the sink and fill with hot water. After a few minutes, or after dinner, use hot water and a sponge to rub off all food particles sticking to the sides. Never use soap or an abrasive pad, as this removes the wok seasoning. Dry the wok over medium heat, then store for future use. Do not add oil to the inside surface, since this eventually turns into a sticky second layer that must be scrubbed off.

PRINCIPLES FOR STIR-FRYING

If stir-frying is new to you, review these principles to ensure success:

Cut the food into smaller pieces that you think necessary. The smaller the food is cut, the more quickly it will cook and the better it will taste.

Cut all ingredients for a recipe to the same shape and size. This ensures even cooking and a more attractive dish.

Never stir-fry more than one pound of meat or seafood in the wok or more than four cups of vegetables. If you double the recipe, have a friend simultaneously stir-fry the second portion in another wok, following your every move.

Do all stir-frying over highest heat, never reducing the heat. This is true even if you have a commercial stove.

Place the ingredients next to the wok in the order in which they will be cooked.

Whenever an ingredient changes color, proceed to the next step. For example, when the stir-fried meat loses its raw color, remove it from the wok. As soon as the ginger and garlic turn white, add the vegetables. When the stir-fried vegetables brighten, pour in the sauce.

Undercook everything. If you find yourself saying, "I'll just cook this a little longer," it's probably already overcooked.

When the sauce comes to a boil, stir in a little of the cornstarch mixture. Add only enough thickener so the sauce lightly glazes the food.

Serve the finished dish immediately.

Asian Ingredients and Shopping Information

The recipes in this book use a small number of Asian herbs, spices, and condiments. Since most Asian supplies sold in our supermarkets are mediocre products, it is worth the effort to acquire the same brands chefs from Asia use. This section describes each of these products and lists the best brands. With the huge influx of Asians during the last decade, nearly every large town across the United States has an Asian market where these products are available. Check your Yellow Pages under "Markets" or "Asian Markets" to locate the nearest one. If this proves unsuccessful, ask at your local Asian restaurant where these supplies are available.

If you are beginning an adventure with Asian cooking, start with the following items, which are the basis for nearly all the recipes in this book. They cost only a few dollars and last indefinitely.

Asian chile sauce
Unsweetened coconut milk
Thai or Vietnamese fish sauce
Hoisin sauce
Thin and dark soy sauces
Oyster sauce
Plum sauce
Rice sticks
Salted black beans
Dark sesame oil

BEAN CURD Known as tofu and referred to by the Chinese as "meat without bones," this is a protein-rich, low-calorie food made from soybeans. The production of bean curd involves adding a coagulant to soy milk, which causes the milk to separate into white curds and clear whey. Gently transferred to cheesecloth-lined boxes, the bean curd is pressed to extract the whey and to form the bean curd into a solid mass. Sold in one-pound blocks immersed in water, Chinese bean curd differs from the Japanese by being more dense, and it is usually cut into four cakes. Bean curd is available in the deli section of most supermarkets, at health food stores, and at all Asian markets. *Storage:* Kept in the refrigerator and submerged under a change of fresh water daily, bean curd will keep for about one week. With longer storage, it begins to take on an unpleasant sour taste. *Best brand:* No preference.

BEAN SAUCE Sometimes called brown-bean sauce, this is a pungent condiment made from yellow beans, flour, salt, and water. While this condiment is sold in the pureed form called "ground bean sauce," purchase only bean sauce containing parts of beans, as this guarantees that top-quality beans have been used to make the sauce. The sauce's unusual taste is not immediately appealing to all, and a little sugar is always added to it to counter the slightly salty taste. *Storage:* Sold in both cans and glass jars. If canned, transfer to a jar and seal tightly. Will keep indefinitely refrigerated. *Substitute:* None. *Best brand:* Koon Chun Bean Sauce, or Yuet Heung Yuen Bean Sauce.

BEAN SPROUTS Called "vegetables for the teeth" by the Chinese, these are three-day-old mung-bean sprouts. They are highly perishable, so if they do not look pearly white, do not buy them. Very fresh bean sprouts add a marvelous crunchy texture to salads or in stir-fry dishes added at the very end of the cooking process. *Storage:* Will keep for two days refrigerated in a plastic food bag lined with paper towels. *Substitute:* Matchstick-cut hothouse cucumber or jicama.

BEAN THREADS Also known as cellophane noodles, glass noodles, transparent noodles, and Chinese vermicelli, these are thin, nearly translucent dried noodles made from ground mung beans. Wrapped tightly together in small bundles, they are soaked in hot water before being cut into shorter lengths and added to soups or spring roll fillings. Bean threads put directly into hot oil from the package will puff up dramatically in size, as rice sticks do. (However, since deep-fried bean threads acquire a stale taste unless eaten immediately, rice sticks are a better choice when you need masses of light, deep-fried noodles to mix into Asian salads.) Bean threads are increasingly stocked in the gourmet section of most supermarkets. *Storage:* Keeps indefinitely at room temperature. *Substitute:* Rice sticks. *Best brand:* No preference.

BLACK BEANS, SALTED Also called fermented black beans, these are small, wrinkled, salted black beans that add a fragrant flavor to sauces. They are always rinsed, coarsely chopped, and then combined with ginger and garlic for stir-fry dishes or rubbed across the surface of fish fillets. *Storage:* Keeps indefinitely at room temperature. *Substitute:* None. *Best brand:* Yang Jiang Preserved Beans with Ginger, or Mee Chun and Koon Chun brands, both of which are available in eight-ounce plastic packages.

BOK CHOY Also known as Chinese cabbage or Chinese chard, bok choy is called "white vegetable" by the Chinese. Its tender, long white stalks and bright green leaves add a subtle flavor to soups and stir-fried dishes. This is one of the Chinese vegetables increasingly stocked by supermarkets across the country. *Storage:* Will keep for one week in the refrigerator. *Substitute:* Chard, tender celery ends, or other quick-cooking vegetable.

CHICKEN BROTH While recipes in this book taste best made with unsalted homemade broth, when necessary, canned broths can be substituted. Or, soak four dried Chinese mushrooms in two cups of hot water for one hour. Strain the liquid and use in place of broth. *Best canned brand:* Swanson Chicken Broth.

CHILE SAUCE, ASIAN Used in this book to make Chinese and Southeast Asian food spicy, this condiment is made with chiles, garlic, salt, and oil. A teaspoon is sufficient to transform a dish from mild to spicy. There are dozens of imported brands variously labeled "chile paste with garlic," "chile sauce," and simply "chile paste or sauce." They are superior in flavor to the spicy Chinese condiment made from soybeans called "hot bean sauce." *Storage:* Keeps indefinitely in the refrigerator. *Substitute:* Use other chile sauces from around the world, or substitute one or more finely minced fresh chiles. *Best brands:* Rooster Brand Delicious Hot Chile Garlic Sauce, sold in nine-ounce clear plastic jars with green tops.

CHILES, FRESH Recipes using fresh chiles in this book usually refer to jalapeño or serrano chiles. Keep in mind that the smaller the chile, the hotter it tastes. The most potent part of the chile is its seeds, so if you want to lessen the spiciness of the dish, either reduce the number of chiles or remove the seeds. To remove the seeds, place your hands in plastic food bags to avoid getting the volatile oil on your skin. Fresh chiles are available at most supermarkets and all Asian markets. *Substitute:* To achieve the same type of spice, substitute ½ teaspoon or more of Asian chile sauce.

CHINESE RICE WINE OR DRY SHERRY While working with Chinese chefs, I have heard some insist on using dry Chinese rice wine, while others adamantly say that the Chinese rice wine imported into this country is of low quality and it is better to use a dry sherry. Over the years of cooking Asian food, I have grown to prefer Chinese rice wine. *Best brand:* Pagoda brand Shao Xing Rice Wine, or Pagoda brand Shao Hsing Hua Tiao Chiew.

CILANTRO Called accurately by the Chinese "fragrant greens," this leafy, small, parsley-like plant with a distinct pungent flavor takes some people several exposures before they really appreciate the delicious taste. Cilantro is sold in Italian, Spanish, and Mexican markets, labeled "fresh coriander," "Chinese parsley," and "cilantro." Unlike all other herbs, the entire cilantro plant, including the stems and roots, which are both flavorful and tender, can be minced along with the leaves. *When available:* Always. *Storage:* Cilantro is highly perishable. Do not wash until ready to use. Wrap roots in a dampened paper towel before refrigerating in a plastic bag. Will last for about five days. *Substitute:* Fresh cilantro has a completely different taste from ground coriander seeds. When unavailable, or for those who do not care for the taste, fresh mint or basil leaves are a good substitute.

COCONUT, FRESH One of the dessert recipes in this book uses fresh coconut milk, which has a subtlety of flavor not present in even the best canned coconut milk from Thailand. Mature coconuts, with a hard brown shell, are available at most supermarkets and all Asian markets. Shake the coconut; it should feel heavy and be filled with liquid (this is coconut water, not milk). After cracking the shell (see page 164), taste a little of the coconut. If it does not have a lovely sweet flavor, it is spoiled and must be discarded. *Storage:* Uncracked coconut can be kept at room temperature for at least one month, and cracked coconut in the refrigerator for one week. *Substitute:* Canned unsweetened coconut milk from Thailand.

COCONUT MILK Excellent canned unsweetened coconut milk is sold in every Asian market. Purchase a Thai brand, the ingredients of which are just coconut, water, and a preservative. Occasionally, the coconut milk is so thick it must be diluted with a little water. *Storage:* Once opened, coconut milk keeps for only a few days in the refrigerator before it takes on a sour flavor. Do not freeze coconut milk, since the oil separates and gives the coconut milk a curdled look. *Substitute:* Fresh coconut milk. *Best brands:* Since there is some variation in flavor among brands, if you live near an Asian market purchase the different brands, then open each, taste, and make a note about the one you prefer. Two good brands are A.C. Products Coconut Milk and Chaokoh Coconut milk, both sold in 5.6-ounce cans.

COOKING OIL Use any flavorless oil that can be heated to very hot without smoking. Good choices are canola, corn, grapeseed, peanut, safflower, and soybean oils.

CORNSTARCH Many of these recipes use a mixture of cornstarch dissolved with an equal amount of cold water to thicken sauces. This ensures that the sauce glazes all the ingredients and prevents any watery liquid from collecting on the bottom of the serving platter. Stirring a few drops of oil into the cornstarch mixture will help prevent the cornstarch from giving the sauce a starchy taste or causing it to lump. Never add all the cornstarch mixture to thicken a sauce. Just add a very small amount and let the sauce come to a low boil; if the sauce does not thicken enough to lightly coat a spoon, then stir in a little more of the mixture.

Substitute: Tapioca starch, rice starch, or potato starch.

CURRY PASTE A blend of many different seasonings mixed with oil, curry paste has numerous advantages over curry powder, including a much more complex taste and a longer shelf life. *Storage:* Once opened, keeps indefinitely at room temperature. *Substitute:* The flavor will not be as complex, but an adequate substitution is to use curry powder and double the amount. *Best brand:* Koon Yick Wah Kee Factory Best Curry, made in Hong Kong, and any good Indian curry paste sold in supermarkets.

CURRY POWDER The quality of curry powder depends on the quality of the whole spices that the manufacturer uses and the freshness of the curry powder. *Storage:* Keep away from heat and on a dark shelf in order to retard its gradual loss of flavor. *Best brands:* In general, curry powders sold by cookware stores and gourmet shops have a superior flavor to brands sold in supermarkets.

EGGPLANT, ASIAN There are dozens of eggplant varieties. By "Asian eggplant," we mean the slender purple- to white-skinned vegetable, about four to eight inches long, that comes from Japan and China. It tastes far superior to the large globe European eggplant. The tender skin makes peeling unnecessary, the virtually seedless interior has no bitter taste, and when sautéed, the eggplant does not absorb large amounts of oil. *Available:* Spring through fall in all Asian markets. Choose the smallest firm eggplants with shiny skins. *Storage:* Lasts for two weeks refrigerated. *Substitute:* Improve all European eggplant recipes by substituting Japanese and Chinese eggplants, and for Asian recipes substitute European globe eggplant only as a last resort.

FISH SAUCE, THAI OR VIETNAMESE This condiment is used in Thai and Vietnamese cooking the way the Chinese use soy sauce. Made by layering fresh anchovies or squid with salt in wooden barrels, it is fermented for several months to produce a watery but flavorful liquid. Always buy fish sauce produced in Thailand or Vietnam; it is superior to those from other countries. Look at each bottle and purchase the light-amber ones rather than the darker products, which will quickly overpower the dish. If you have a doubt about the quality of the fish sauce, purchase several brands and do a taste test; use the one that is least salty. *Storage:* Once opened, lasts indefinitely at room temperature. *Substitute:* None. *Best brand:* Three Crab Brand, Phu Quoc Flying Lion Brand, or Tiparos Fish Sauce.

FIVE-SPICE POWDER A powdered blend of various spices including anise, fennel, cinnamon, Sichuan pepper, and cloves, this is a great favorite of the Cantonese for marinades, poultry, and fish. Five-spice powder is sold in one-ounce bags in Asian markets and by some supermarkets in the spice section. *Storage:* Keeps indefinitely at room temperature if tightly sealed in a jar. *Substitute:* None. *Best brand:* Five-spice powder sold by Asian markets is the best.

GINGER, CRYSTALLIZED These are slices of fresh ginger that are candied and coated with sugar. Their sweet, sharp ginger flavor makes them an excellent addition chopped and sprinkled over ice cream, or as a candy served with fresh fruit. Crystallized ginger sold by American markets is often stale. Test by pressing the package; the ginger slices should feel soft. *Available:* In most supermarkets and all Asian stores. *Storage:* Keeps indefinitely at room temperature sealed in a jar. *Substitute:* None.

GINGER, FRESH Absolutely indispensable for Asian cooking, these pungent and spicy-tasting knobby brown rhizomes are sold by supermarkets in the produce section. Buy firm ginger with smooth skin. Never peel ginger. Cut off and discard the exposed end. Cut into very thin slices crosswise (so that the minced pieces will have no fiber), then finely mince by hand or in an electric minichopper. *Storage:* Store ginger in a dark cupboard, where it will stay fresh for up to a month. This is better than placing ginger in the refrigerator, where the moisture quickly causes it to spoil, or freezing ginger, which affects the flavor. When the skin begins to wrinkle and the root softens, discard. *Substitute:* There are no substitutes, since ground ginger has a different taste, while preserved and crystallized ginger is too sweet.

HOISIN SAUCE A thick, sweet, spicy, dark brown-red condiment, hoisin sauce is customarily spread across pancakes for mu shu pork and Peking duck; it flavors many stir-fry dishes, and is the base for delicious Chinese barbecue sauces. Made with soybean flour, chiles, garlic, ginger, and sugar, it is one of the Chinese condiments most loved by Americans. It is sold by Asian markets in both glass jars and cans. *Storage:* Once opened, keeps indefinitely at room temperature. *Substitute:* None. *Best brand:* No Asian condiment varies so much in quality from brand to brand. Buy only Koon Chun Hoisin Sauce.

JICAMA This brown-skinned Mexican root vegetable has a sweet, white interior with a crunchy texture. It makes a great addition to salads. Ranging in size from a fist to a cantaloupe, jicama is sold by many supermarkets. Peel with a knife before using. *Storage:* Jicama will last for two weeks in the refrigerator if you cover the cut surface with plastic wrap. *Substitute:* Fresh water chestnuts are a good substitute for jicama in salads, but jicama is not a good substitute for fresh water chestnuts in cooked dishes, since jicama does not maintain its crunchy texture during cooking.

LEMONGRASS This is one of the most important seasonings for Thai and Vietnamese cooking. Available in most Asian markets, lemongrass is a three-foot-long greenish plant having an eight-inch woody stem and long, slender leaves. The woody stem, having a faint lemon flavor, is finely minced and added to dishes the same way you would use minced ginger, or it is cut on a sharp diagonal into half-inch pieces and added to dishes such as stews or soups, which gently simmer on the stove. Added in large pieces, lemongrass is meant to flavor the dish and not to be eaten. Soaked in hot water, the leafy ends make lemongrass tea, to settle an upset stomach. Lemongrass grows very easily in a temperate climate. You can either plant store-bought lemongrass that still has some of the roots attached, or purchase lemongrass in the herb section of some nurseries. *Storage:* Lemongrass just cut from the garden has a subtle flavor that disappears within two days, even with refrigeration. *Substitute:* Powdered lemongrass, available at most Asian markets, has little taste, so you would be better off substituting a little grated lemon peel, although the flavor is not quite the same.

MONOSODIUM GLUTAMATE (MSG) A white crystalline powder sold under various names such as Accent and Ajimoto, it is used by chefs of little skill to rejuvenate food of poor quality. Sold in large plastic bags in Asian markets, MSG has sadly become a staple "seasoning" in many Chinese restaurant dishes, and is the cause for throbbing headaches referred to as Chinese restaurant syndrome. Chinese cooks who take pride in their cuisine regard monosodium glutamate as a crutch. It is neither recommended nor used in this book.

MUSHROOMS, DRIED BLACK CHINESE Chinese markets sell a wide variety of dried mushrooms that are the equivalent of Japanese dried shiitake mushrooms. Do not confuse these with the rippled-edged "black fungus," which has no flavor and a totally different texture. Chinese black mushrooms, when softened in hot water, add a wonderful meaty flavor to soups, stir-fried dishes, and stews. The thicker the cap, the higher the quality and the more expensive the mushroom. To use, soak mushrooms in a generous amount of hot water. When they soften, cut off and discard the stems. Strain the mushroom-flavored water through a fine-mesh sieve and use it as a substitute for chicken broth. A similar Japanese variety called dried forest mushrooms are sold in many supermarkets. *Storage:* Sealed in jars, they last indefinitely unrefrigerated. *Substitute:* For stir-fried dishes, soups, and stews, substitute fresh mushrooms, although the flavor will not be as intense. For spring roll and dumpling fillings, fresh mushrooms are not a good substitute, since they do not have the density of the dried variety.

MUSHROOMS, ENOKI These are little clumps of mushrooms on long, threadlike stems joined together at the base. Their wonderful sweet smell and delicate look make them a great addition to salads and as a garnish. To use, cut off the base and separate the mushroom threads. Do not wash. *Storage:* Sold in small plastic bags at good supermarkets, they will stay fresh for about four days, refrigerated. *Substitute:* None.

MUSHROOMS, OYSTER These mushrooms are light gray and have a fairly large trumpet shape with very delicate edges. They are sold in four-ounce boxes in the produce section of good supermarkets. Because of their fragile texture, oyster mushrooms are best used in salads or very briefly cooked in stir-fry and sauté dishes, rather than being added to stews or soups. *Storage:* Transferred to a paper bag, they will last for about five days in the refrigerator. *Substitute:* Other types of fresh mushrooms, but never use the canned oyster mushrooms sold in Asian supermarkets.

MUSHROOMS, FRESH SHIITAKE Fresh Japanese forest mushrooms, which are never sold at Asian markets because of their expense, are appearing increasingly in supermarkets. Fresh shiitake mushrooms possess an incredible fragrance and are delicious sautéed in butter as an accompaniment for grilled meats, in stir-fried dishes, simmered in cream sauces, and thinly sliced for salads. They are not good, however, chopped and used in dumpling fillings, since they do not have the intense flavor and density of dried mushrooms. Fresh shiitake mushrooms are completely clean and should never be washed. Discard the tough stem before using the cap. *Storage:* Kept in a paper bag, they will last up to two weeks in the refrigerator. *Substitute:* Dried Chinese mushrooms, although the flavor is not quite the same.

MU SHU WRAPPERS These are very thin flour tortillas that are served with one of the most famous northern Chinese stir-fry dishes, mu shu pork. They make a wonderful wrapping for all stir-fry dishes, and to cradle slices of barbecued meat seasoned with spoonfuls of salsa. Our version of mu-shu wrappers, called Peking Chive Pancakes, appears on page 150. Frozen mu-shu wrappers are available at most Asian markets. However, many of the store-bought wrappers are thick and coarse tasting. *Substitute:* Fresh flour tortillas. *Best brand:* Republic Frozen Food, Moo-Shu Wrapper, Product of the Philippines.

NOODLES, CHINESE DRIED, SPAGHETTI STYLE Thin dried spaghetti-type noodles are sold in one- to five-pound boxes at all Asian markets. They are inexpensive, cook quickly, and have a nice firm texture. *Storage:* Indefinitely at room temperature. *Substitute:* Any dried thin spaghetti-style noodle.

NOODLES, SOBA These are one of my favorite noodles and I eat them almost every day for lunch. The size of spaghetti and made from buck-wheat flour, they cook very quickly in a large amount of rapidly boiling water. *Storage:* Indefinitely at room temperature. *Substitute:* Any dried thin spaghetti-style noodle.

OYSTER SAUCE This is also called oyster-flavored sauce. You can visit the beaches near Hong Kong and see huge piles of shucked oysters used for making this oyster ketchup. Oyster sauce gives dishes a marvelous rich taste without a hint of its seafood origins. A pinch of sugar is usually added in dishes using oyster sauce to counteract the slight salty taste. *Storage:* Keeps indefinitely in the refrigerator. *Substitute:* None. *Best brands:* Lee Kum Kee Oyster Flavored Sauce, Old Brand.

PLUM SAUCE This chutney-like condiment, a great favorite of Cantonese cooks, is made with fresh plums, apricots, garlic, red chiles, sugar, vinegar, salt, and water. It is different from duck sauce, which is made with plums, apples, and spices. The thick consistency and sweet, spicy flavor of plum sauce makes it an ideal addition to barbecue sauces and as a dip for crisp, deep-fried wontons or chilled shrimp. It is available in cans and glass jars at all Asian markets and in many supermarkets. *Storage:* If canned, once opened, transfer to a glass jar and seal. Keeps indefinitely unrefrigerated. *Substitute:* None. *Best brand:* Koon Chun Plum Sauce.

RADICCHIO Radicchio is a small, tightly bunched head of red-leaf chicory. Torn or slivered in salads, or sautéed, its bittersweet flavor and bright color have made this one of the new favorites of chefs at top restaurants. It is available at many supermarkets in the produce section. *Storage:* Stored in a plastic food bag in the refrigerator, it will last for ten days. *Substitute:* While the unusual taste and color of radicchio cannot be duplicated, you can substitute another green, such as endive.

RICE, WHITE LONG-GRAIN The Chinese eat long-grain white rice, while the Japanese prefer the stickier short-grain white variety. Neither of these should be confused with the inferior-tasting converted and minute brands, which are precooked and dried at the factory before packaging. White rice is available at all Asian markets and all supermarkets, sold in small clear plastic bags. *Storage:* Keeps indefinitely at room temperature. *Substitute:* None.

RICE STICKS Rice sticks are long, thin, dried rice-flour vermicelli. Rice sticks put directly from the package into hot oil instantly puff up into a huge white mass many times their original size. They are an essential ingredient in many Chinese salads, and are used as a bed for stir-fried dishes. For cooking instructions, see page 46. Rice sticks are available at all Asian markets and most supermarkets. *Storage:* Keeps indefinitely at room temperature. *Substitute:* None. *Best brand:* Sailing Boat Brand Rice Sticks or Lucky Boy Rice Sticks.

RICE VINEGAR Clear Japanese rice vinegar with its mild flavor is particularly good for pickling, salad dressings, and seafood sauces. Avoid inferior rice vinegars labeled "seasoned" or "gourmet," which indicate that sugar and often monosodium glutamate have been added. Nor should Japanese rice vinegar be confused with Chinese rice vinegar, which has too mild a taste for these recipes. Rice vinegar is available at all Asian markets and most supermarkets. *Storage:* Keeps indefinitely at room temperature. *Substitute:* Possibly Champagne vinegar, although this has a sharper taste. *Best brand:* Marukan Rice Vinegar.

SESAME OIL, DARK Sold in small bottles, dark Asian sesame oil is a nutty golden-brown oil made from crushed toasted sesame seeds. It is used only as a seasoning and never as a cooking oil, since its low smoking temperature will cause it to ignite. This is an ingredient, like hoisin sauce, that varies greatly in quality. Unfortunately, most sesame oil sold by American supermarkets has a harsh taste, so look for sesame oil in Asian markets. *Storage:* At room temperature it will last for at least a year before turning rancid, and will last indefinitely in the refrigerator. *Substitute:* None. *Best brand:* Kadoya Sesame Oil tastes outstanding. Avoid Dynasty Sesame Oil.

SESAME SEEDS, WHITE Sold in the spice section of every supermarket, white sesame seeds are far less expensive purchased at Asian markets. They are used in many recipes, toasted until light golden in an ungreased skillet. *Storage:* Since white and toasted sesame seeds become stale at room temperature or when refrigerated, keep them in the freezer.

SICHUAN PEPPERCORNS Labeled Szechuan pepper, wild pepper, fagara, and *fa tsiu,* these are little reddish-brown seeds from the prickly ash tree. They have a beautiful aromatic flavor without any of the spiciness of black and white peppercorns. They are available at cookware stores, gourmet shops, and at all Asian markets, sold in two-ounce plastic bags.

To use, place Sichuan pepper in an ungreased skillet and toast until the pepper smokes slightly. Transfer to a coffee or spice grinder and pulverize. Tip into a sieve with a medium mesh and shake. The light brown shells remaining in the sieve have no taste and should be discarded. *Storage:* Store ground Sichuan pepper in a small glass spice jar. The aromatic flavor will last for about six months. *Substitute:* None.

SNOW PEAS These flat, light-green pods are sold year-round in many supermarkets. If snow peas are soft when purchased, soaking them in cold water for 30 minutes restores their firm texture. To use, snap off and draw the stem end down the ridge to remove the fiber. Whether stir-fried, blanched for salads, or added to soups, snow peas are perfectly cooked as soon as they turn bright green. *Storage:* Keep for at least a week in a plastic food bag in the refrigerator. *Substitute:* Sugar snap peas, or another quick-cooking vegetable.

SOY SAUCE, DARK Sold in bottles of varying sizes, dark soy sauce, also called heavy or black soy sauce, is light soy sauce with the addition of molasses or caramel. Chefs use it to add a richer flavor and color to sauces. Never confuse this with "thick" soy sauce in jars, which is a syrup like molasses that will ruin the taste of any recipe in this book. One way to tell the difference between dark and light soy is to shake the bottle. Dark soy sauce will coat the sides of the bottle whereas the more watery thin soy sauce will not. *Storage:* Once opened, keeps indefinitely at room temperature. *Substitute:* None. *Best brand:* Mushroom Soy Sauce.

SOY SAUCE, LIGHT This is the most common soy sauce used in Chinese cooking. Made from soybeans, roasted wheat, yeast, and salt, good light soy sauce is available at all Asian markets and most supermarkets. It is used as a table condiment, in stir-fried dishes, and in soups where a light color and delicate taste are desired. If you are concerned about sodium, it is better to reduce the quantity of light soy sauce in the recipe rather than use low-sodium brands. *Storage:* Once opened, keep indefinitely at room temperature. *Substitute:* None. *Best brands:* Koon Chun Thin Soy Sauce, Superior Soy Sauce, and Kikkoman Soy Sauce. When buying Superior Soy Sauce, look carefully at the label, for the manufacturer bottles another soy called Soy Superior, which is a dark soy sauce.

SPRING ROLL SKINS These are paper-thin skins made from flour and water. Sold twenty-five to a package in the freezer section of all Asian markets and labeled "spring roll skins," "Shanghai wrappers," "lumpia skins," and, confusingly, "egg roll skins," they are far thinner and become much more crisp when deep-fried than the thick egg-noodle skins sold in American supermarkets called "egg roll skins." To use, defrost for an hour, then loosen one corner and peel off one skin at a time. Stack the skins and cover with a towel until ready to assemble the spring rolls. You will find that while the skins appear to be tightly stuck together, they are very strong and will not tear as you pull them apart. *Storage:* Kept in the freezer tightly wrapped, they last indefinitely. Spring rolls can be thawed and refrozen repeatedly without affecting their quality. *Substitute:* None. *Best brands:* Those imported from Hong Kong and Menlo Wrappers.

WATER CHESTNUTS The size of an English walnut, water chestnuts are botanically no relation to our chestnuts. They are a black-skinned water bulb grown in southern and eastern China. Called "horses' hooves" by the Chinese, they are often covered with a thin layer of mud to prevent them from drying out. Their very sweet taste and crunchy texture are as different from that of their canned cousins as fresh asparagus is from canned. On the West Coast, fresh water chestnuts come from Hong Kong, while along the East Coast, they are grown in Florida. Fresh water chestnuts are available only in a few large Chinatown communities, but are sold throughout the year. When buying fresh water chestnuts, squeeze each one and discard any that are soft; these are rotten in the center. Under cold running water, peel off the skins using a small knife. They can be used raw in salads, added to soup or stir-fried dishes, minced for dumpling fillings, or dipped in chocolate. Their wonderful taste and texture remain unchanged despite lengthy cooking. *Storage:* Unpeeled water chestnuts last for two weeks wrapped in a plastic bag and refrigerated. *Substitute:* If you are not fond of canned vegetables, do not use canned water chestnuts! In dumpling fillings, substitute minced carrot. For stir-fried dishes, just substitute another fresh vegetable. In Asian salads, substitute jicama.

WONTON SKINS Measuring about three inches square, wonton skins are thin egg-noodle wrappers. They are sold by every Asian market and in many supermarkets. Most supermarkets also sell round "gyoza skins." These are just wonton skins with the corners trimmed away. Purchase the thinnest ones, preferably fresh and not frozen. The latter, which dry out and become brittle in the freezer, tend to tear when folded for dumplings. *Storage:* Keeps for two weeks in the refrigerator if tightly sealed. *Substitute:* None.

Conversion Chart

LIQUID MEASURES

Fluid Ounces	U.S. Measures	Imperial Measures	Milliliters	Fluid Ounces	U.S. Measures	Imperial Measures	Milliliters
	1 tsp	1 tsp	5		1 tsp	1 tsp	5
1/4	2 tsp	1 dessertspoon	7	18	2 1/4 cups		500, 1/2 liter
1/2	1 tbs	1 tbs	15	20	2 1/2 cups	1 pint	560
1	1/4 cup	4 tbs	15	24	3 cups or 1 1/2 pints		675
4	1/2 cup or 1/4 pint		110	25		1 1/4 pints	700
5	1/4 pint or 1 gill	140		27	3 1/2 cups		750
6	3/4 cup		170	30	3 3/4 cups	1 1/2 pints	840
8	1 cup or 1/2 pint		225	32	4 cups or 2 pints or 1 quart		900
9	250, 1/4 liter			35		1 3/4 pints	980
10	1 1/4 cups or 3/4 pint	1/2 pint	280	36	4 1/2 cups		1000, 1 liter
12	1 1/2 cups	3/4 pint	420	40	5 cups or 2 1/2 pints	2 pints or 1 quart	1120
16	2 cups or 1 pint		450	48	6 cups or 3 pints		1350

SOLID MEASURES

U.S. and Imperial Measures — Ounces	Pounds	Metric Measures — Grams	Kilos	U.S. and Imperial Measures — Ounces	Pounds	Metric Measures — Grams	Kilos
1		28		18		500	1/2
2		56		20	1 1/4	560	
3 1/2		100		24	1 1/2	675	
4	1/4	112		27		750	3/4
5		140		28	1 3/4	780	
6		168		32	2	900	
8	1/2	225		36	2 1/4	1000	1
9		250	1/4	40	2 1/2	1100	
12	3/4	340		48	3	1350	
16	1	450		54		1500	1 1/2
				64	4	1800	

OVEN TEMPERATURE EQUIVALENTS

Fahrenheit	Gas Mark	Celsius	Heat of Oven	Fahrenheit	Gas Mark	Celsius	Heat of Oven
225	1/4	107	very cool	375	5	190	fairly hot
250	1/2	121	very cool	400	6	204	fairly hot
275	1	135	cool	425	7	218	hot
300	2	148	cool	450	8	232	very hot
325	3	163	moderate	475	9	246	very hot
350	4	177	moderate				

TERMINOLOGY EQUIVALENTS

U.S.	British	U.S.	British
Eggplant	Aubergine	Confectioners' sugar	Icing sugar
Zucchini	Courgette	Broil	Grill
Heavy cream	Double cream	Broiler	Grill
Sugar, granulated sugar	Castor sugar	Skillet	Frying pan

Artwork Credits

page 1: ceramic by Helen Slater and Robin Spear
page 2: tile background by Country Floors
page 5: teapot by Jeff Irwin
page 11: "Bungalow Teapot" by David Gurney
pages 14–15: platter by David Foglia
page 22: platter by Helaine Melvin
page 26: plate by Mesolini Glass
page 31: chopsticks by Sue Dorman; plate by Bill Goldsmith/Limoges; background painting by Teri Sandison
page 33: background by Jeff Stillwell
page 48: plates by Christina Salusti
page 51: plate by George Sowden/Swid Powell; flatware by Sakasi
pages 54–55: plate by Sepanski
page 58: "Pepper and Flowers Teapot" by David Gurney
page 59: background by Jeff Stillwell
page 62: platter by Kerry Feldman; background painting by Teri Sandison
pages 66–67: glassware by John Gilvey; ladle by Nutmeg Pewter
page 70: plate by Barbara Schuppe
page 71: bowl by Barbara Schuppe; background place mat by Judith Klein
page 74: bowls by Barbara Schuppe; background painting by Teri Sandison
page 78: Candelabra by Ries Niermi
page 79: background by Jeff Stillwell
pages 82–83: glass by David Foglia
page 87: plate by Kerry Feldman; background place mat by Judith Klein
page 89: plate by Les Lawrence; background set design by Jeff Stillwell
page 88: teapot by Beverly Saito
page 90: tile background by Country Floors
page 95: plate by Sasaki; background drawing by Teri Sandison

page 96: plate by James Gorman; background drawing by Teri Sandison
page 101: platter by Barbara Schuppe; glasses by Magic Sands; background painting by Teri Sandison
page 104: plates by Barbara Schuppe; background drawing by Teri Sandison
pages 108–109: plates by Annie Glass
page 112: platter by Kerry Feldman; silk-screened place mat by Judith Klein
pages 116–117: platter by Nancy Toler; glasses by Fineline Studio; background painting by Teri Sandison
page 121: platters and mugs by Luna Garcia; background painting by Jeff Stillwell
page 124: teapot by Jeff Irwin
page 125: platter by Nancy Toler; background painting by Teri Sandison
pages 128–129: plates by Sugahara
page 132: "Bird and Pepper Vase" by David Gurney
page 136: pot by Holly Collins
page 137: platter by Artquake; background painting by Teri Sandison
page 140: platter by James Gorman; glasses by Magic Sands; background painting by Teri Sandison
page 144: ceramic cup by Reed Keller
page 145: platter by Barbara Schuppe
pages 148–149: tile background by Country Floors
pages 152–153: glasses by Rede Guzzini
page 156: plates and teapot by Barbara Schuppe; background place mat by Judith Klein
page 161: plate by Terry Shapiro; silver flatware by Georg Jensen
page 168: plate by Lyn Evans
Back jacket: platter by Artquake; background painting by Teri Sandison

Acknowledments

So many people contributed their special gifts to this book. Our publisher, Lena Tabori, urged us on to complete the manuscript. This book glows because of the efforts of our food stylists. Norman Stewart is a European-trained chef who is known for his beautiful food design. After styling our first book, *Pacific Flavors,* Norman joined our team for this book. He works as a food stylist for top photographers and film companies in Los Angeles and New York. Jean E. Carey, Los Angeles-based food stylist, who also styled *Pacific Flavors,* specializes in creative food design for print and film. She has been the production coordinator for fifty-two half-hour cooking shows for television and does product conceptualization and design for major food corporations. Stephen Shern is a food stylist for major food publications, top photographers, ad agencies, and production companies in both Los Angeles and New York. His fifteen years of experience as a professional chef combined with his eye for design are the foundation for his unique style. Fred Walker received his training as a chef at the Culinary Institute of America. He combines his passions for food and design through his beautifully styled food. Originally based in Philadelphia, he now works in Los Angeles for top photographers in film and still photography.

Many friends helped bring this book into print. Our attorney, Susan Grode, helped us refine the book proposal. Many thanks to talented book designer Melanie Random, copyeditor Eugenia Leftwich, and to the tireless efforts and many insights of our editor, Amy Schuler, at Stewart, Tabori & Chang. The following chefs and friends contributed great assistance and ideas: Mark Dierkhising, Roger Hayot, and Grant and Sharon Showley. Thank you.

We found rich sources of props and accessories for the photography at several Los Angeles art galleries. We especially want to thank Carol Sauvion at Freehand and Stephen and Diane Reissman of Tesoro Collection for their generosity and support. We were always thrilled by wonderful creations at the Wild Blue and New Stone Age galleries. Thank you also to Lynne Deutch Ltd., By Design, Solo Lo Mejor, and L.A. Hotlites.

After the recipes were tested at home and taught in cooking classes, they were given a final review by the following cooks. This book gained much from your special insights. Thank you, Florence Antico, Peggy and David Black, Pamela Blair, Jo Bowen, Yvonne Caan, Bill and Lynda Casper, Karen and Don Cerwin, Jan Debnam, Cary Feibleman, Peter Feit, Diane Ganzell-Brown, Sharie and Ron Goldfarb, Robert Gordon, Blanche Gottlieb, Donna Hodgens, Tim Howe and Ann Janss, Nancy Huntsinger, Diana Kleinmann, Joy and John Knox, Jeannie Komsky, Susan Krueger, Patty Lewis, Kris Livos, Betty Mandrow, Bernard Menard, Patricia Niedfelt, Michele Nipper, Joanne Persons, Roy Pingo, Jeannie Riley, Joe Rooks, Kathleen Sands, Michele Sciortino, Jerry Sexton, Mary Jo and Paul Shane, Ellie Shulman, Philip Stafford, Elaine Stein, Suzanne Vadnais, Susan Vollmer, Ruth Walker, Sharon Whelan, and Robert Wills. Thank you all for your help.

Index

Page numbers in *italics* refer to illustrations.

Appetizers:
Asian summer rolls, 37
Asian tropical gazpacho, 70, *71*
chile shrimp with basil, *2, 25*
chilled crab with ginger, 38
crisp spring rolls with lettuce and mint wrap, *26–27,* 28-29
firecracker dumplings, *26–27, 27*
ginger gravlax, 24
goat cheese with Pacific flavors rub, 21
grilled shiitakes with lime and ginger, 19
mu shu pork bonanza, 123
Pacific flavors salad, *44–45,* 46
Pacific-style tamales, *140,* 141
peanut satay sauce, 41
sashimi spring rolls, 20
scallop ravioli in saffron–caviar sauce, 30, *31*
smoked baby-back ribs with Pacific flavors barbecue sauce, 105
spicy marinated mussels, *22, 23*
spicy scallop salsa with ginger, *14–15,* 19
spicy stir-fry beef, 118
stir-fried shrimp with garlic and chiles, 111
stuffed shiitake mushrooms, *14–15,* 18
Tex-Mex won tons with new age guacamole, *32, 33*
Thai fried dumplings, 36
Thai salmon satay, 16
Thai shrimp pizza, 34
Thai-high barbecued chicken, 103
wok-seared beef in endive cups, 35
yakitori, 17
see also salads
apricot sweet and sour sauce, 41
Asian:
barbecued salmon, 92
fruit salad, 65
grilled chicken salad, 52

ingredients and shopping information, 172–183
lamb wraps, 120
mushroom pasta, 142
noodle magic, 138
polenta, 131
roasted red pepper salad, 50
seasonings, mesquite barbecued lamb with, 107
shrimp Louis salad, 60
summer rolls, 37
tropical gazpacho, 70, *71*
wraps, spicy noodles with, 70, *71*
avocado:
Asian tropical gazpacho, 70, *71*
chilled, soup with ancho chile jam, 80
tropical paradise salad, 58, *59*
see also new age guacamole

Barbecued:
lamb, mesquite, with Asian seasonings, 107
salmon steaks with spicy herb coconut sauce, 85
salmon, Asian, 92
veal chops with macadamia nuts, *96, 97*
vegetables with Pacific flavors, *128–129,* 130
barbecued chicken:
spicy chicken wraps, 124, *125*
Thai-high, 103
barbecue sauce, 107
smoked rib-eye steaks with ginger-mango salsa, 94, *95*
barbecue sauce, Pacific flavors, 105
barbecue sauce, vegetable, 130
basil:
and cilantro, curried clams with, 114
chile shrimp with, 25
cilantro butter, 84
sautéed crab with lemongrass sauce and, *90, 91*
bean(s):
black, sauce, shrimp in, 127
curd (tofu), 172
salted black, 173
sauce, 172–173
bean sprouts, 173
bean threads, 173
beef:

salad, South Seas, 64
smoked rib-eye steaks with ginger-mango salsa, 94, *95*
spicy stir-fry, 118
tenderloin with Thai green curry sauce, 106
wok seared, in endive cups, 35
berries:
fresh, with coconut cream and chocolate, *168,* 169
Zinfandel macerated strawberries, warm polenta cake with, 163
see also raspberry Cabernet Sauvignon sauce
black beans, salted, 173
sauce, shrimp in, 127
bok choy, 173
bouillabaisse, Thai, *66–67,* 68
bread(s)
California cornbread, 151
new wave garlic, *74,* 147
broth, chicken, 173
homemade, 69
brownies, orange ginger, *156,* 158
butter:
cilantro-basil, 84
herb, steamed lobster with, *82–83,* 84
lemon-ginger, 84
butter sauce:
ginger-cilantro sauce, grilled swordfish with, 88

Cabernet Sauvignon raspberry sauce, 160
Caesar salad, crazy, *62,* 63
Cakebread Winery's fallen chocolate soufflé, 167
California cornbread, 151
caramel fudge tart with crumble crust, 164
cashews and scallops in tangerine sauce, 113
caviar-saffron sauce, scallop ravioli in, 30, *31*
champagne rice pilaf, 143
cheese *see* goat cheese
chicken:
broth, homemade, 69
chiu chow lemon, 99
firecracker dumplings, *26–27, 27–28*
roast, with Zinfandel

mushroom sauce, 100, *101*
salad, Asian grilled, 52
salad, with spicy peanut glaze, 61
Sichuanese, with eggplant, 122
southern fried, Pacific style, 102
spicy, wraps, 124
spicy, with lettuce cups, *108–109,* 110
Thai-high barbecued, 103
yakitori, 17
chicken broth, 173
homemade, 69
chile(s)
ancho jam, chilled avocado soup with, 80
fresh, 174
garlic and, stir-fried shrimp with, 111
sauce, Asian, 174
shrimp with basil, 25
chilled avocado soup with ancho chile jam, 80
chilled crab with ginger, 38
chilled yellow tomato soup with ginger, 76
chiu chow lemon chicken, 99
chive Peking pancakes, *137,* 150–151
chocolate:
caramel fudge tart with crumble crust, 164
chip-macadamia nut cookies, 155
decadence, 166
drizzle, mango ice cream with, 157
magic mousse, 154
mudslide cookies, 165
orange ginger brownies, 158
soufflé, Cakebread Winery's fallen, 167
warm crème brûlée, 162
chocolate Grand Marnier sauce:
lemon ice cream with, 159
coconut cream, with fresh berries, *168,* 169
cilantro:
and basil, curried clams with, 114
basil butter, 84
ginger butter sauce, grilled swordfish with, 88
coconut:

cream, with fresh berries
and chocolate, *168,* 169
curry soup explosion, 78, *79*
fresh, 174
milk, 175
noodle toss, crazy, 132
shredded, 174
conversion chart, 184
cookies:
chocolate chip-macadamia
nut, *152–153,* 154
chocolate mudslide, 165
cooking oil, 175
corn:
California cornbread, 151
new age guacamole, *33,* 42,
121, 140
Pacific-style tamales, *140,*
141
Tex-Mex salad with ginger
dressing, 47
cornbread, California, 151
cornstarch, 175
crab:
chilled, with ginger, 38
sautéed, with basil
lemongrass sauce, 91
crazy Caesar salad, *62, 63*
crazy coconut noodle toss, 132
crisp pan-fried trout, 93
crisp spring rolls with lettuce
and mint wrap, *26–27,* 27–28
curry:
clams, with basil and cilantro,
114
dip, Thai red, 43
paste, 175
powder, 175
soup explosion, coconut, 78
Thai green, sauce, beef
tenderloin with, 106
custards:
chocolate decadence, 166
coconut cream with fresh
berries and chocolate, *168,*
169

Desserts:
Cakebread Winery's fallen
chocolate soufflé, 167
caramel fudge tart with
crumble crust, 164
chocolate chip-macadamia
nut cookies, *152-153,* 155
chocolate decadence, 166
chocolate mudslide cookies,

165
coconut cream with fresh
berries and chocolate, *168,*
169
lemon ice cream with
chocolate Grand Marnier
sauce, 159
magic mousse, *152–153,* 154
mango ice cream with
chocolate drizzle, *156,* 157
orange ginger brownies, *156,*
158
raspberry Cabernet
Sauvignon tart, 160, *161*
warm chocolate crème
brûlée, 162
warm polenta cake with
Zinfandel macerated
strawberries, 163
dim sum, *see* appetizers
dips:
apricot sweet and sour sauce,
41
ginger mustard sauce, 42
new age guacamole, *33,* 42,
121, 140
peanut satay sauce, 41
plum lemon dip, 40
Thai dipping sauce, 43
Thai red curry dip, 43
tropical fruit salsa, 39, *121,*
140
see also sauces
dry sherry, 176
dumplings:
firecracker, *26–27,* 27–28
Thai fried, 36
see also won ton

Eggplant:
oriental, 176
with Sichuanese chicken, 122
enoki mushrooms, 179

Firecracker dumplings, *26–27,*
27–28
fish:
Asian barbecued salmon, 92
barbecued salmon steaks
with spicy herb coconut
sauce, 85
crisp pan-fried trout, 93
ginger gravlax, 24
grilled swordfish with ginger-
cilantro butter sauce, 88, *89*
sauce, 176

sashimi spring rolls, 20
Thai bouillabaisse, *66–67,* 68
Thai salmon satay, *14–15,* 16
wild rice seafood soup, 73
see also shellfish
five-spice powder, 176
flower-blossom squid, 115,
116–117
fried:
dumpling, Thai, 36
southern, chicken, Pacific
style, 102
trout, crisp pan-, 93
see also stir-fry
fruit:
Asian tropical gazpacho, 70
salad, Asian, *48,* 65
salsa, tropical, 39, *121, 140*
tropical paradise salad, 58
Zinfandel macerated
strawberries, warm
polenta cake with, 163
see also lemon, mango

Garlic bread, new wave, *74,*
146
ginger:
chilled crab with, 38
chilled yellow tomato soup
with, 76
cilantro butter sauce, grilled
swordfish with, 88, *89*
crystallized, 177
dressing, Tex-Mex salad with,
47
fresh, 177
goat cheese salad with
macadamia nuts and,
48, 49
gravlax, 24
grilled shiitakes with lime
and, 19
lemon butter, 84
mustard sauce, 42
orange brownies, *156,* 158
peanut noodle salad, 56
spicy scallop salsa with, 19
ginger-mango salsa, 94, *125*
Sichuan veal meat loaf, 98
smoked rib-eye steaks with,
94
spicy chicken wraps, 124
glass noodle(s), 176
goat cheese:
salad, with ginger and
macadamia nuts, *48, 49*

with Pacific flavors rub, 21
won ton soup, 77
Grand Marnier:
chocolate decadence, 166
magic mousse, *152–153,* 154
Grand Marnier chocolate sauce,
159
gravlax, ginger, 24
grilled:
chicken salad, Asian, 52
shiitakes with lime and
ginger, 18
swordfish with ginger-
cilantro butter sauce,
88, *89*
guacamole, new age, *33,* 42,
121, 140

Hoisin sauce, 177
homemade chicken broth, 69
hors d'oeuvres, *see* appetizers
hot and sour Sichuan tomato
soup, *74, 75*
hot potatoes two ways, 133

Ice cream:
lemon, with chocolate Grand
Marnier Sauce, 159
mango, with chocolate
drizzle, *156,* 157
ingredients, Asian, and
shopping information,
172–183

Jade noodles, 139
jicama, 177–178

Lamb:
mesquite barbecued, with
Asian seasonings, 107
spicy orange, with peppers
and onions, 126
wraps, Asian, 120, *121*
lemon:
chiu chow chicken, 99
ginger butter, 84
ice cream with chocolate
Grand Marnier sauce, 159
plum dip, 40
lemongrass, 178
crab with basil and, 90, *91*
lettuce:
and mint wrap, crisp spring
rolls with, *26–27,* 27–28
crazy Caesar salad, *62, 63*
cups, spicy chicken with,

108–109, 110
goat cheese salad with ginger
and macadamia nuts,
48, 49
wok-seared beef in
endive cups, 35
lobster, steamed, with herb
butters, 84

Macadamia nut(s):
barbecued veal chops
with, 96, 97
chocolate chip cookies,
152–153, 155
goat cheese salad with
ginger and, 48, 49
magic mousse, 152–153, 154
mango(es):
ice cream with chocolate
drizzle, 156, 157
salad, Thai, 57
tropical paradise salad, 58
mango-ginger salsa, 94, 125
meat loaf, Sichuan veal, 98
meats:
Asian lamb wraps, 120, 121
barbecued veal chops with
macadamia nuts, 96, 97
beef tenderloin with Thai
green curry sauce, 106
mesquite barbecued lamb
with Asian seasonings, 107
mu shu pork bonanza, 123
Sichuan veal meat loaf, 98
smoked baby-back ribs with
Pacific flavors barbecue
sauce, 105
smoked rib-eye steaks with
ginger-mango salsa, 94
South Seas beef salad, 64
spicy orange lamb with
peppers and onions, 126
spicy stir-fry beef, 118
wok-seared beef in endive
cups, 35
yakitori, 17
Melrose mushroom salad,
53, 54–55
mesquite barbecued lamb with
Asian seasonings, 107
miso, 178
monosodium glutamate (MSG),
178
mousse, magic, 152–153, 154
mushrooms:
dried black Chinese, 178–179

enoki, 179
grilled shiitakes with lime
and ginger, 19
oyster, 179
pasta, Asian, 142
roast chicken glazed with
Zinfandel sauce, 100, 101
salad, Melrose, 53, 54–55
stuffed shiitake, 18
three, soup, 81
mu shu pork bonanza, 123
mussels, spicy marinated, 22, 23
mustard ginger sauce, 42

New age guacamole, 33, 42,
121, 140
new wave garlic bread, 74, 147
noodles:
coconut curry soup
explosion, 78, 79
three mushroom soup, 81
noodle(s), Chinese dried
spaghetti-style, 179
Asian mushroom pasta, 142
jade, 139
magic, Asian, 138
salad, peanut ginger, 56
toss, crazy coconut, 132, 133
noodle(s), glass, 173
noodle(s), rice stick, 116–117,
180
Pacific flavors salad, 46
spicy, with Asian wraps, 136
noodles, soba, 179
nuts:
peanut ginger noodle salad,
56
peanut satay sauce, 41
scallops and cashews in
tangerine sauce, 112, 113
Sichuan veal meat loaf, 98
see also macadamia nut

Orange ginger brownies, 156,
158
oriental:
sesame oil, 176
shrimp Louis salad, 60
oyster mushrooms, 179
oyster sauce, 180

Pacific flavors:
barbecue sauce, 105
dipping sauces, 40–43
rub, goat cheese with, 21
salad, 44–45, 46

with barbecued vegetables,
128–129, 130
Pacific-style, southern fried
chicken, 102
Pacific-style tamales, 140, 141
Pacific-style wild rice, 146
pancakes, see Peking chive
pancakes
pasta, see noodle
peanut:
ginger noodle salad, 56
glaze, spicy, chicken salad
with, 61
satay sauce, 41
Peking chive pancakes, 137,
150–151
pepper, spicy orange lamb with
onions and, 126
pepper, red roasted, salad,
Asian, 50, 50–51
pepper, sweet, Thai pork
tenderloin with, 119
peppercorns, Sichuan, 181
pilaf, champagne rice, 143
pizza, Thai shrimp, 34
plum sauce, 180
lemon dip, 40
polenta:
Asian, 131
cake, warm, with Zinfandel
macerated strawberries,
163
pork:
mu shu, bonanza, 123
smoked baby back ribs with
Pacific flavors barbecue
sauce, 105
tenderloin, Thai, with sweet
peppers, 119
potatoes, hot, two ways, 133
poultry see chicken

Radicchio, 180
raspberry(ies):
Cabernet Sauvignon tart, 160
caramel fudge tart with
crumble crust, 164
chocolate decadence, 166
coconut cream with fresh
berries and chocolate, 169
ravioli, scallop, in saffron-caviar
sauce, 30, 31
really risqué rice, 144, 145
rib-eye steaks with ginger-
mango salsa, 94, 95
ribs, smoked baby back, with

Pacific flavors barbecue
sauce, 105
rice:
pilaf, champagne, 143
really risqué, 144, 145
white long-grain, 180
wild, Pacific style, 146
wild, seafood soup, 73
rice stick(s), 116-117, 180
Asian grilled chicken salad,
52
flower blossom squid, 115
Pacific flavors salad, 46
rice vinegar, 180–181
roast chicken with Zinfandel
mushroom sauce, 100, 101
roasted red pepper salad, Asian,
50, 51

Saffron-caviar sauce, scallop
ravioli in, 30, 31
salad(s):
Asian fruit, 48, 65
Asian grilled chicken, 52
Asian roasted red pepper, 50,
50–51
Asian shrimp Louis, 60
chicken, with spicy peanut
glaze, 61
crazy Caesar, 62, 63
goat cheese, with ginger and
macadamia nuts, 48, 49
Melrose mushroom, 53,
54–55
Pacific flavors, 44–45, 46
peanut ginger noodle, 56
South Seas beef, 64
Tex-Mex, with ginger
dressing, 47
Thai mango, 57
tropical paradise, 58
salmon:
Asian barbecued, 92
ginger gravlax, 24
satay, Thai, 14–15, 16
steaks, barbecued, with spicy
herb coconut sauce, 85
sashimi spring rolls, 19
sauces:
apricot sweet and sour, 41
Cabernet Sauvignon, 160
chocolate drizzle, 157
chocolate Grand Marnier,
159
ginger mustard, 42

new age guacamole, *33, 42, 121, 140*
Pacific flavors, 105
peanut satay, 41
plum lemon dip, 40
raspberry Cabernet
    Sauvignon, 160
spicy herb coconut, 85
Thai dipping, 43
vegetable barbecue, 130
see also dips
scallop(s):
    and cashews in tangerine
        sauce, *112, 113*
    ravioli, in saffron-caviar
        sauce, *30, 31*
    spicy salsa, with ginger, 19
    thread soup, 72
sautéed crab with basil
    lemongrass sauce, *90,* 91
seafood:
    flower blossom squid, 115,
        116–117
    soup, wild rice, 73
    steamed lobster with herb
        butters, *82–83,* 84
    see also fish; shellfish
sesame oil, dark, 181
sesame seeds, white, 181
shellfish:
    Asian shrimp Louis salad, 60
    Asian summer rolls, 37
    cashews and scallops in
        tangerine sauce, *112, 113*
    chile shrimp with basil, 25
    chilled crab with ginger, 38
    crisp spring rolls with lettuce
        and mint wraps, *26–27,
        27–28*
    curried clams with basil and
        cilantro, 114
    sautéed crab with basil
        lemongrass sauce, *90,* 91
    scallop thread soup, 72
    scallop ravioli in saffron-
        caviar sauce, *30, 31*
    scallops and cashews in
        tangerine sauce, *112, 113*
    shrimp in black bean sauce,
        127
    spicy scallop salsa with
        ginger, 19
    spicy marinated mussels,
        22, 23
    steamed lobster with herb
        butters, *82–83,* 84

stir-fried shrimp with garlic
    and chiles, 111
Thai bouillabaisse, *66–67,* 68
Thai fried dumplings, 36
Thai sautéed shrimp, 86, *87*
Thai shrimp pizza, 34
sherry, dry, 176
shiitake mushrooms, 179
    grilled, with lime and
        ginger, 19
    stuffed, 18
shopping information, Asian
    ingredients, and, 172–183
shrimp:
    Asian summer rolls, 37
    chile, with basil, 25
    in black bean sauce, 127
    Louis salad, Asian, 60
    pizza, Thai, 34
    stir-fried, with garlic and
        chiles, 111
    Thai fried dumplings, 36
    Thai sautéed, 86, *87*
Sichuan:
    chicken with eggplant, 122
    hot and sour tomato soup, 75
    peppercorns, 181
    veal meat loaf, 98
smoked baby back ribs with
    Pacific flavors barbecue
    sauce, 105
smoked rib-eye steaks with
    ginger-mango salsa, 94, *95*
snow peas, 181
southern fried chicken, Pacific
    style, 102
soup(s):
    Asian tropical gazpacho, 70,
        71
    chilled avocado, with ancho
        chile jam, 80
    chilled yellow tomato, with
        ginger, 76
    coconut curry, explosion, 78,
        79
    goat cheese won ton, 77
    homemade chicken broth, 69
    hot and sour Sichuan tomato,
        74, 75
    scallop thread, 72
    Thai bouillabaisse, *66–67,* 68
    three mushroom, 81
    wild rice seafood, 73
South Seas beef salad, 64
soy sauce, 182
spicy chicken with lettuce cups,

108–109, 110
spicy chicken wraps, 124
spicy marinated mussels, *22, 23*
spicy noodles with Asian wraps,
    136
spicy orange lamb with peppers
    and onions, 126
spicy scallop salsa with ginger,
    19
spicy stir-fry beef, 118
spring rolls:
    crisp, with lettuce and mint
        wrap, *26–27, 28–29*
    sashimi, 20
spring roll skins, 182
sprouts, bean, 173
    peanut ginger noodle salad,
        56
squid, flower blossom, 115,
    116–117
steaks, smoked rib-eye, with
    ginger-mango salsa, 94, *95*
    barbecued salmon, with spicy
        herb coconut sauce, 85
steamed lobster with herb
    butters, *82–83,* 84
stir-fry(ied):
    beef, spicy, 118
    garden vegetables, 134–135
    shrimp, with garlic and
        chiles, 111
    spicy chicken with lettuce
        cups, *108–109,* 110
    Thai pork tenderloin with
        sweet peppers, 119
    wok-seared beef in endive
        cups, 35
stir-frying and woks, 170–171
strawberries, Zinfandel
    macerated, warm polenta
    cake with, 163
stuffed shiitake mushrooms,
    14–15, 18
swordfish, grilled, with ginger-
    cilantro butter sauce, 88

Tamales, Pacific-style, *140, 141*
tangerine sauce, scallops and
    cashews in, *112, 113*
tart:
    caramel fudge, with crumble
        crust, 164
    raspberry Cabernet
        Sauvignon, 160
Tex-Mex won tons with new
    age guacamole, 32

Tex-Mex salad with ginger
    dressing, 47
Thai:
    bouillabaisse, *66–67,* 68
    dipping sauce, 43
    fried dumplings, 36
    mango salad, 57
    pork tenderloin with sweet
        peppers, 119
    red curry dip, 43
    salmon satay, 16
    sautéed shrimp, 86
    shrimp pizza, 34
Thai-high barbecued chicken,
    103
    spicy chicken wraps, *124,* 125
three mushroom soup, 81
tomato(es)
    sweet and sour soup,
        Sichuan, *74, 75*
    tropical paradise salad, 58, *59*
    yellow, chilled, soup, with
        ginger, 76
tropical paradise salad, 58, *59*
tropical salsa, 39, *121, 140*
trout, crisp pan-fried, 93

Veal:
    chops, barbecued, with
        macadamia nuts, *96,* 97
    meat loaf, Sichuan, 98
vegetables:
    barbecued, with Pacific
        flavors, *128–129,* 130
    stir-fried garden, 134–135

Warm chocolate crème brûlée,
    162
warm polenta cake with
    Zinfandel macerated
    strawberries, 163
water chestnuts, 182–183
wild rice, Pacific style, 146
wild rice seafood soup, 73
woks and stir-frying, 170–171
wok-seared beef in endive cups,
    35
won ton(s):
    goat cheese, soup, 77
    skins, 183
    Tex-Mex, with new age
        guacamole, 32

Yakitori, *14–15,* 17

■

Book design by Melanie Random
Production by Amanda Freymann

Composed in Adobe Mistral
and Simoncini Garamond

Printed and bound by
Toppan Printing Company, Ltd.,
Tokyo, Japan

■